Contents

Chapter 1: Design Tools

- Flow Charts 5
- Mind maps 6
  - Library Mind Maps 7
- Tunnel Timeline 7
- Presentation Mind Map 8
- Key Characteristics of mind maps 8
- Visualisation Diagrams 9
  - Visualisation Diagrams Summarised 10
- Wireframe Diagrams 11

Chapter 2: Human Computer Interface (HCI) in everyday life 12

- What is an HCI? 12
  - Why do we need an HCI? 13
  - Where can an HCI be used? 13
- Application of an HCI 14
- Hardware Considerations 15
- Display Types 15
- Command Line Interface (CLI) 15
  - Menu Driven Interface 17
- Resources 21
- Display Screen 21
- External peripherals 22
- Memory and Storage 24
- Primary Storage 24
- Secondary Storage 27
- Processing Power 28
- System Requirements 28
- Software Considerations 29
  - Operating Systems 29
- Digital Platforms 30
  - Databases 30
  - Mobile App 31
  - Spreadsheet 32

  Websites Vs. Mobile Apps 32

 User interaction methods 34

Chapter 3: Data and testing 35

 Information Vs Data 35

 Using data in the real world 36

  Data Types 36

 Validation and Verification 37

  Data Validation Tools 37

  Data Collection Methods 38

Chapter 4: Storage 39

 Logical Storage Devices 39

 Physical Storage Devices 40

 Internal Physical Storage 40

 External Physical Storage 40

Chapter 5: Application of testing to a range of contexts 41

 Importance and purpose of testing 41

 Test Data 41

 Types of testing 42

Chapter 6: Cyber-security and legislation 43

 Threats 43

 Hacking 44

  Black Hat Hacking 44

  Grey Hat Hacking 44

  White Hat Hacking 45

 Social engineering 46

 Malware 47

 Cyber Security Impacts 48

 Preventing Threats 49

  Physical Protection Methods 49

  Dual Prevention Methods - Both logical and Physical 50

  Logical Prevention Methods 50

  Secure Destruction of Data 51

 Legislation 52

  Computer Misuse Act 1990 52

  GDPR 2016 53

Copyright, Designs and Patents Act 1988 54
Freedom of Information Act 2000 55
Health and Safety at Work Act 2000 56
Legislation Summary 57

Chapter 7: Digital Communications 58

Types of Digital Communications 58
    Audio 58
    Collaboration Tools 59
    Infographics 59
    Social Media 60
    Video 61
    Voice over Internet Protocol (VoIP) 62

Distribution Channels 63
    Cloud 63
    Email 63
    Multimedia 63

Connection Methods 64
    4G / 5G 64
    Bluetooth 64
    Mobile Wi-Fi hotspots 65
    Wi-Fi 65
    Wired 66
    Fibre 68

Chapter 8: The Internet of Everything (IoE) 69

The Four Pillars of the IoE 69
    People 69
    Data 70
    Process 70

Internet of Things and The Internet of Everything 70
IoE digital interactivity 71
Applications of the IoE 72

R070: Using Augmented Reality to present Information 73

What is Augmented Reality? 73
AR In Architecture 74
AR in Education 75

Augmented Reality in the Entertainment Industry 76
    Gaming 76
    AR in Movies/TV and Film 77
AR in Retail 78
AR in lifestyle 79
AR in applications 81
Negative Impacts of AR 81
Types of Augmented Reality and user interaction 82
    Layers/User Interaction 85

Glossary 86
Index 93

Chapter 1: Design Tools

Flow Charts

A flow chart is a diagrammatical representation workflow or a process. The workflow is a term used within business and IT that means the direction in which the work completed will flow.

An example of workflow is below. In this example, how to make a cup of tea, the workflow progresses from not having any components for the cup of tea to having a cup of tea by the end.

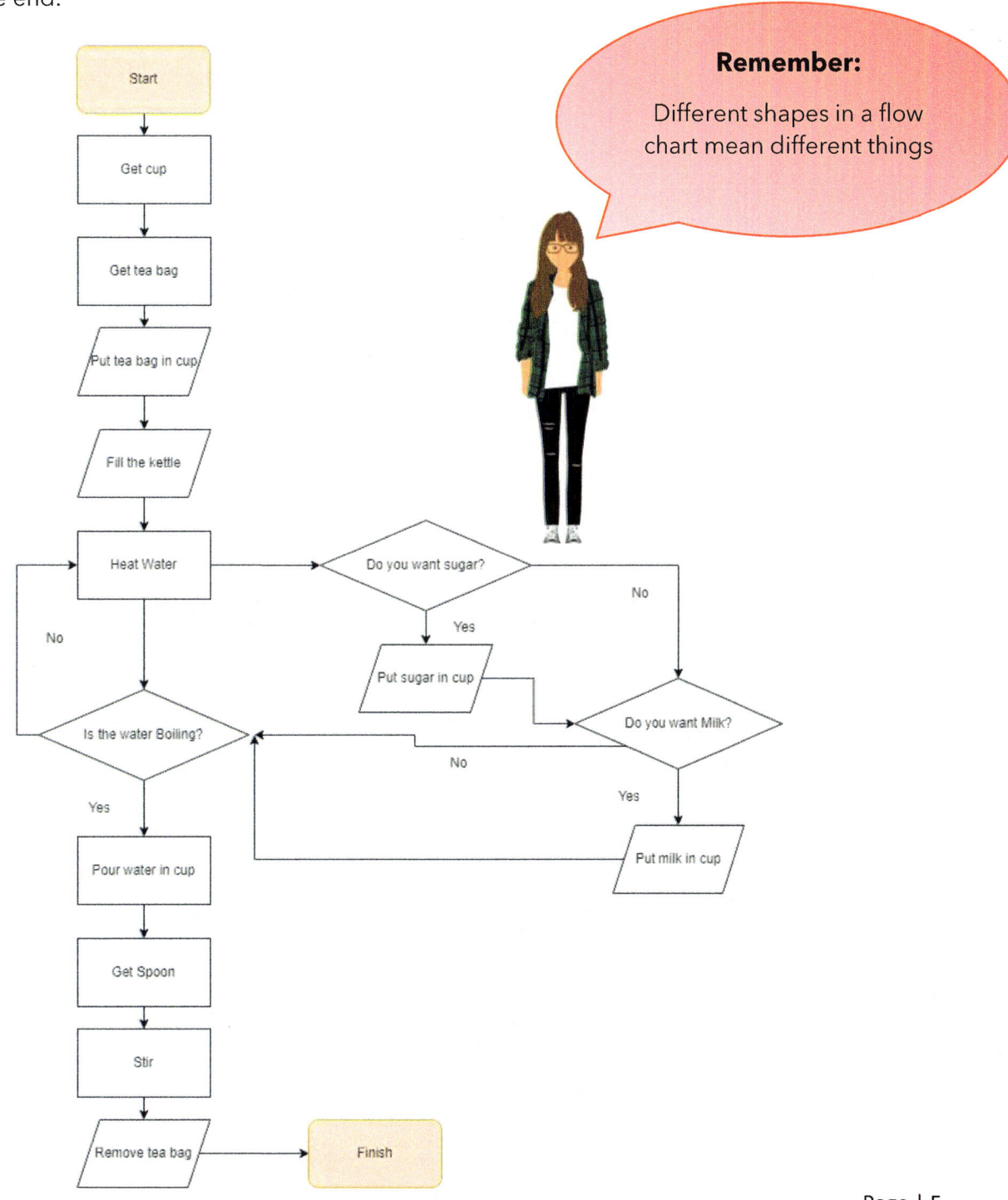

A flow chart can also be described as a diagrammatical representation of an algorithm, it is a step-by-step approach to solving a task or problem. A flow chart will show the steps needed to complete the solution to a problem. It does this by using a variety of different box shapes.

Task:

1. What are the symbols/shapes associated with the following flow chart functions? Start/End, Input/Output, Process, Decision
2. Draw a flow chart for brushing your teeth or another daily routine.
    a. Have a peer follow your flow chart and make changes accordingly.

Mind maps

A mind map is a tool used in the design process of many industries. It is one of the design tools that you are likely to be most familiar with. Often known by several different names, essentially, they are a diagrammatical representation of information or idea. They are useful tools to see the relationships between different pieces of information. They provide a bird's eye view of a concepts proposed solution and allow a team of designers to 'map' out their solution.

There are several different types of mind maps. The three you need to know are:

- Library
- Tunnel timeline
- Presentation

```
Key Vocabulary:

• Node
• Tunnel Timeline
• Library Mind Map
• Presentation Mind Map
• Branch
```

Library Mind Maps

Library mind maps are the most common mind maps, these are the mind maps you are likely to have used in a range of scenarios throughout your schooling. They are used by designers to quickly organise a collection of ideas or information in a what that is easy to see and visualise. A library mind map can be used in a range of situations, for big projects to little activities.

Library mind maps. Like most mind maps, consist of shapes, linked together with lines showing connections.

TASK:

Create a library mind map, with a person in your class, to plan a trip to your local town, cinema, bowling or sporting event. Consideration needs to be given to cost (budget), transport, timings (schedule) and food/drink (resources).

Did you know?

The shapes on a mind map are known as nodes!

Tunnel Timeline

A tunnel timeline is named as such because they are designed to narrowly take you on a journey to achieve your goal. The purpose of this mind map is to visualise success. The main topic of the mind map is the outcome that the user wishes to get to. Each subtopic on the journey through the tunnel represents a pathway needed to achieve the goal or the end outcome.

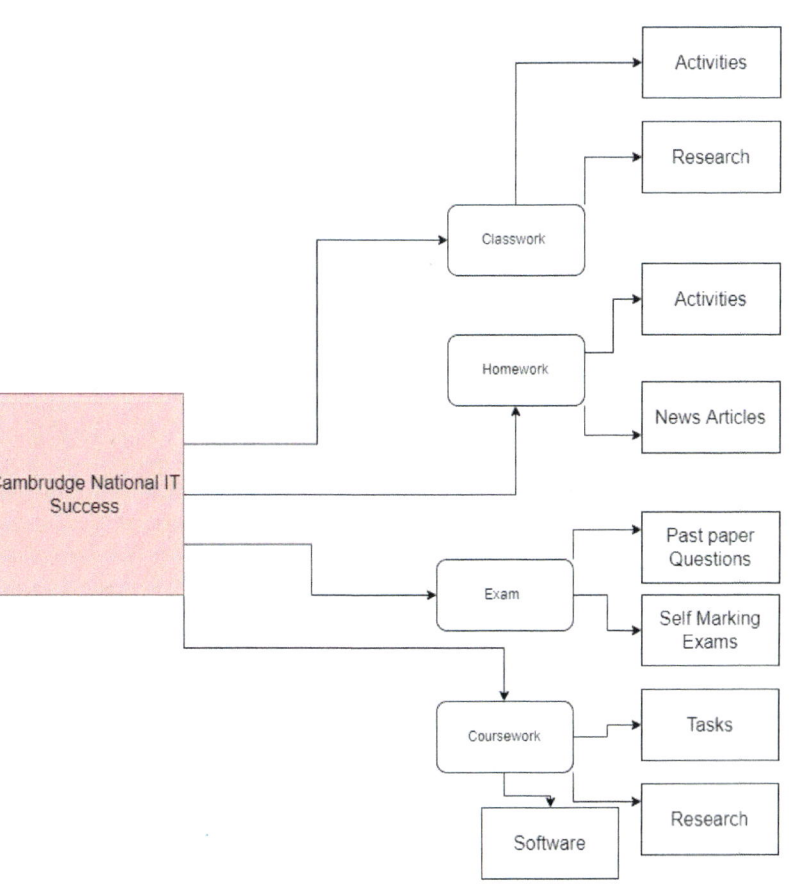

Presentation Mind Map

This type of pf mind map is used to present the process of an idea to the audience. Presentation mind maps illustrate the way that the project goes in order to track the steps. Therefore, the focus of a presentation mind map is the audience instead of the topic.

How the information should be positioned in the map depends on whether the audience can understand it or not. If the audience can follow with the way you are presenting, then the map is well structured. Thus, you presentation can be well accepted by the audience.

Key Characteristics of mind maps

Mind Map Type	Example Software	Advantages	Disadvantages
Library Mind Map	Coggle Mindly MindMup MindMeister Stormboard Ayoa MindNode SimpleMind	Can be used in a variety of scenarios Used widely – many people can make them Easy to create on paper and digitally	Can be confusing and messy for a person to read Can be hard to follow Can be chaotic – generated as ideas form in a person's mind
Tunnel Timeline Mind Maps		Can clearly show the goal of a project Breaks down the project into smaller tasks Can be read by anyone – doesn't rely on author explanation	Needs the author to understand how to create the mind map Requires specialist software if created on a PC Can take time to create Hard to create if the end goal is not clear
Presentation Mind Map		Can be used to clearly present an idea/concept to a client Easy to see and has a clear structure Decomposes a problem into smaller tasks Clear pathways/lines through the map	Can take extra time as they are often created, neatly, from a library mind map. Can be still confusing for someone who isn't the author without the author present to explain.

Visualisation Diagrams

Visualisation diagrams are powerful design tools. They pre-date computers and can be used both digitally and in a paper form to represent an idea/concept visually to key stakeholders.

Visualisation diagrams are often a rough drawing or sketch of what the final product is intended to look like. They will have annotations to describe the design ideas. It is important to remember that a visualisation diagram does not require any artistic skill and is more of a concept generation which can then be used to help an artist visualise the final product.

It is intended to demonstrate the layout and content of the product that is being illustrated. A company might produce several drafts to demonstrate ideas to their client and from these drafts the client might choose the draft they like the most.

There must be sufficient information in the visualisation diagram for the client to decide about their preferred design.

Visualisation diagrams are only valid for static designs, that is an image or product that does not move. It is, therefore, relevant for designs such as a magazine cover, a DVD cover, or an image for a website. It would not be suitable for a video or an animation.

Visualisation diagrams are also used in a variety of industries including aviation design, automotive design and clothing design. They allow the client or the end user to see what the product might look like at a very early stage of the design process.

```
Key Vocabulary:

• Visualisation Diagram
• Static
• Concept
• Sketch
• Client
```

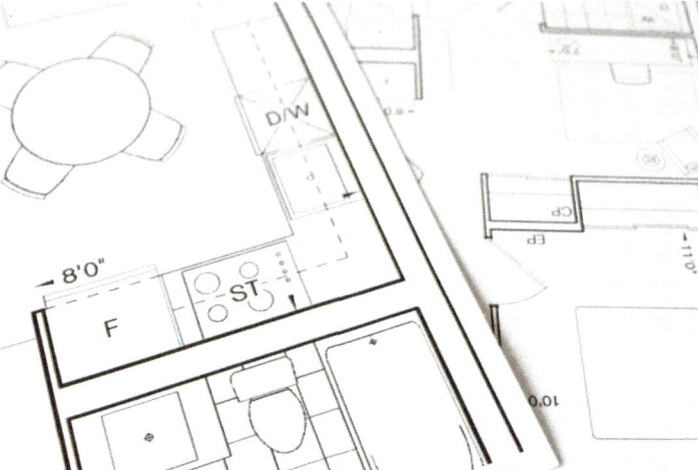

Image shows diagrammatical drawing showing a visualisation of a new home.

Visualisation Diagrams Summarised

Purpose:

1. Plan the layout of a static product or still image in a visual manner
2. To show how a finished item might look like

Uses:

- CD/DVD cover design
- Poster, such as for a film, event, leaflet or advertisement
- A single game scene of display of a single scene
- Comic book page layout
- Physical product design such as clothing, cars, or technology items.

What do they contain?

- Multiple images, layout and positions of items.
- Colours and colour schemes
- Position and styles of text
- Fonts, font colours and size
- Notes as annotations which provide additional information
- Size if images
- Position of logos, icons and other items needed by the client

Task:

1. Using a piece of paper, and colouring pencils. Draw a new trainer, car or games console. Ensure you use the list above to ensure it contains enough detail for a designer to pick it up and design your product. **TIP:** Ensure you include annotations and descriptions
2. Using a web browser and search engine of your choice. Find three visualisation diagrams of three different products.
   Support: Search for – Trainer visualisation diagram, Plane visualisation diagram or car visualisation diagram

Wireframe Diagrams

A wireframe diagram is a systems designer's best friend! It allows the systems design team to 'map' out where digital assets are going to be placed on the screen.

But it isn't only used by system architects. It can be sued, in a paper form, to represent the layout of a user interface (UI). The wireframe consists of simple lines and shapes used as place holders to signify an asset's location on a page.

Websites, apps, software and anything with a UI will require a wireframe before production begins.

Image showing a hand drawn visualisation diagram for a website.

Uses	Software	Advantages	Disadvantages
Websites	Gliffy	The layout is clear to the designer/developer	Very basic. They don't explain interactions between the user and the UI. They can miss important information required by the end user to make the project a success.
Applications	Draw.io		
Operating Systems			
	Wireframes are so simple they could be created in many software packages that allow the user to draw shapes!	Easy to read and understand	
		Give the client the opportunity to see what the UI will look like before it is developed.	

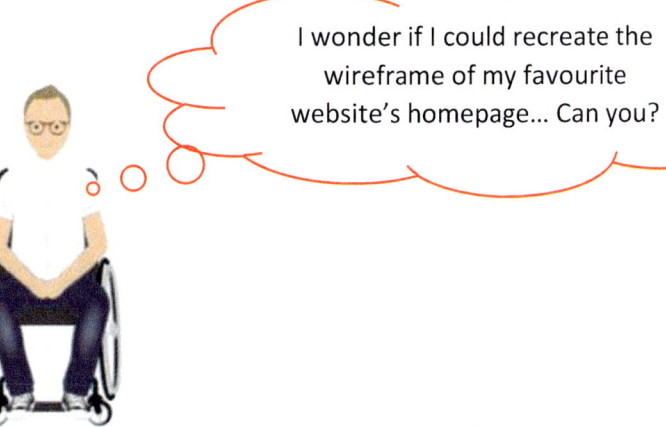

I wonder if I could recreate the wireframe of my favourite website's homepage... Can you?

Chapter 2: Human Computer Interface (HCI) in everyday life

What is an HCI?

Computer systems are relatively young, with the first digital computer making its way into the world in the 1970's. Since then, we have seen rapid growth in computer evolution to smart phones, tablets, games consoles and other devices that allow user interaction.

Any device will require human interaction of some sort. Whether that is an embedded system such as a washing machine with a series of dials, or a tablet which requires electrical signals from your finger to create a selection. The interface used within all devices that require human interaction is referred to the Human Computer Interface, or HCI for short. The HCI is vitally important to a device's success, poor HCI's can lead to people not wanting to use a device and good, intuitive, HCI's can lead to lifelong repeat customers or users for a technology company.

HCI, which started being discussed in the 1960's is the research undertaken by technology companies to focus on the interfaces between people (the user) and computers (the machine). Through the history of computer science researchers have observed humans and the way they interact with technology to be able to make advancements that benefit the daily usage of digital devices and systems.

Task:

Windows, Apple macOS, Apple's iOS, Android, Chrome, Ubuntu, Linux and Unix operating systems and software all require a HCI. This HCI will impact the design of the operating system and software. Therefore, the HCI is different on an iPhone to an iPad and again to a Mac.

Complete the table below:

System	HCI Image	Suggestion as to why this impacts design	Pros and Con's
Windows 98			
Windows XP			
Windows 8		Menu based system, like a tablet, removal of Start Menu. Likely because many people had started to use tablets at this time of release.	Many people struggled with the loss of the start menu. It was able to be used on a tablet and a desktop
Windows 10			
iOS 1.1.4			
iOS 14.8.1			
Android 1.0			
Android 12.0			

Why do we need an HCI?

Did you know? The word Computer means to count!

Without a HCI the human would struggle to interact with a device. In the early days of computer science, the HCI was nothing more than lines of code on the screen, think The Matrix © only less futuristic. Humans typed in lines of code to ask the computer to complete something.

There are a multitude of ways a computer can be interacted with by a human. Buttons and dials are mechanical whereas most are digital. Having an HCI, that is well designed, thought out and utilised means that a user can interact with the system you have built easily, confidently and successfully. Most commonly, our modern day HCI's use the WIMP model. WIMP stands for:

1. **Windows** - Individual screens that open and close upon request
2. **Menus** - These can drop down, like file or insert, pop up like a start menu on a Windows machine, or pop out like on a mobile phone
3. **Icons** - Little images that signify a product or document. These appear on your home screen or desktop. Examples include app images and program shortcuts. They give the user an indication of what they are going to open before it is opened.
4. **Pointers** - This is your mouse, stylus, pen or finger! They allow you to select, highlight and navigate the computers interface.

Where can an HCI be used?

On any digital device requiring human interaction. Some digital devices work on their own, in solitary isolation, things like your alarm clock (if it is digital) or your cars ECU. But most digital 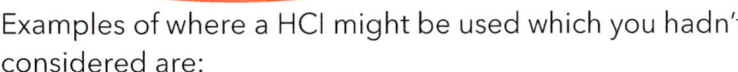 devices require a human input.

Can you list all the devices in your home where a HCI has been considered and therefore you use?

Examples of where a HCI might be used which you hadn't considered are:

- Smart watch
- Sat Nav
- Car Information Management System
- Microwave
- Washing Machine

Embedded systems require human input to and so their HCI must be considered when designing the product.

Application of an HCI

HCI's are used in a wide range of areas and industries. Some will sue digital devices similarly and others will use them in completely different ways. Recently, in 2017, McDonalds ™ introduced large screens to order food from as opposed to visiting a customer service agent at the counter, similarly, most cinemas, train stations and bus stations have a facilitate to book tickets via a kiosk in a central location.

Each of these digital devices require a HCI and so considerations over the user's interaction, and input need to be made.

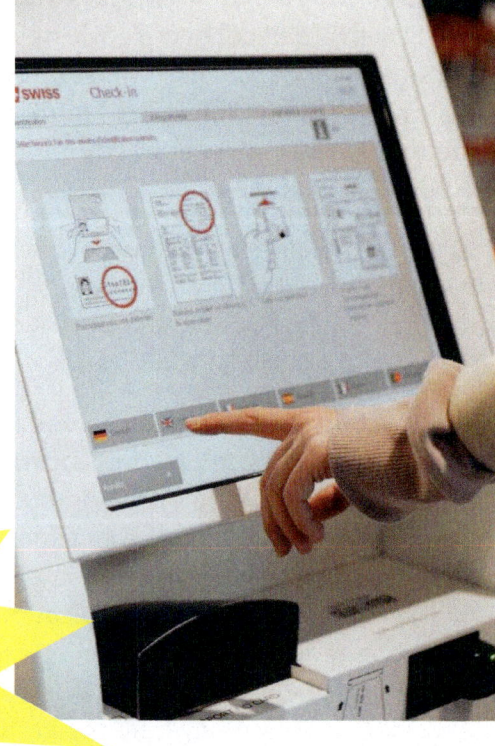

Research

Ticketless plane travel with easyJet at London Gatwick

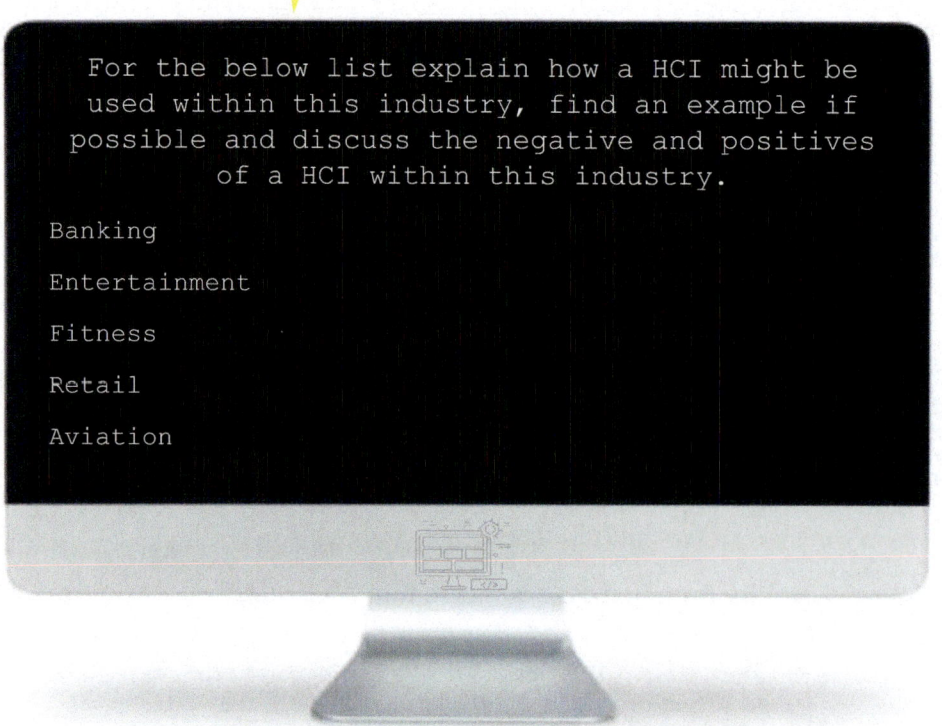

For the below list explain how a HCI might be used within this industry, find an example if possible and discuss the negative and positives of a HCI within this industry.

Banking

Entertainment

Fitness

Retail

Aviation

Hardware Considerations

Before starting to design a HCI the designer must know the hardware that the device will be using. This is important because it will influence the HCI's design and functionality. The may hardware considerations are:

Display Types

The types of interfaces can be broken down into four categories.

- Command Line Interface (CLI)
- Menu Driven interface
- Graphical User Interface (GUI)
- Natural Language Interface

Command Line Interface (CLI)

Command Line Interface (CLI) the CLI displays a prompt on a screen to the user. The user then types a command on their screen, using their keyboard. The computer takes the command, executes it and returns a result.

In the 1960's, CLI was the only way humans could interact with commuters. The terminal, or computer, would have text displayed on the screen and the user would respond to the text with commands, that's how it got its name of command line interface.

As time progressed other interfaces started to be used instead of CLI, in the 1970's and 1980's systems such as Unix and PC systems such as MS-DOS and Apple DOS all used command line as their interface and interaction with humans.

Today CLI is often used by software developers and system administrators to configure computers, install software and access features that are sometimes not accessible through other interfaces.

Here is an example of how a user might navigate their folders (directories) with command line commands:

```
C:\Users\myuser>cd ..
C:\Users\>cd ..
C:\>
```

Task:

Can you describe/guess the basic Microsoft Windows CLI commands below:

Command	Description
dir	
cd pathname	Change directory (folder) in file system
cd \	
cd ...	
copy	
move	
type *filename*	
mkdir or md	

Menu Driven Interface

The user has a series of menus which contain buttons to choose from. The user will select by highlighting a button/option and selecting it.

Simple menu

In this form of menu driven interfaces the user is shown a simplified menu on the screen from which they select an option. One menu often leads to another sub menu. The screen might not be only made up of buttons and a text box might be on the screen to direct and instruct the user.

An example of this in everyday life would be an ATM or bank machine where the user is presented with menus to complete their transaction

Full screen menu

Full screen menu interfaces and screen menu interfaces are difficult to often spot the difference. Unlike a screen menu, a full screen menu will take up the entire screen and options within the menu may include images to help the user understand the description on the menu.

An example of this is the full screen menu in McDonalds ™ or on the vintage iPod range where the user only has a menu system to see and nothing else.

Menu bar

A menu bar is a set of options on the screen where when pressed/clicked by the user a menu appears usually either a s a drop down or pop-up menu. A very common menu bar that you will have used will be the menu bar at the top of Microsoft Office products.

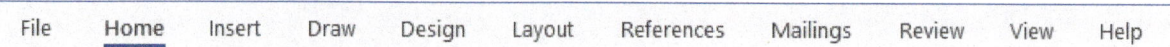

Common features of a menu bar are:

- Ease of use – they are easy for the user to navigate and find their desired option
- User friendly – often menu bars are user friendly and are structured similarly meaning that the user feels confident and at ease with the navigation of the system.

Negatively, they can be confusing and irritating to the user if there are too many sub menus that they need to navigate to find a single option or if they are badly structured or not structured in a logical way.

With menu bar interfaces a great deal of attention must be paid to the names given to options for the user to click.

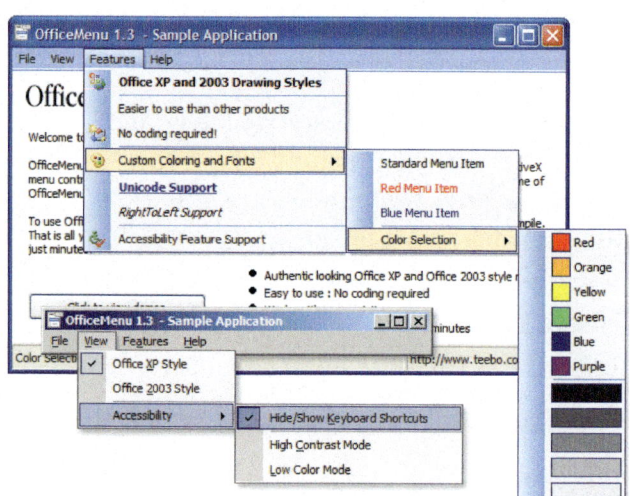

Key Vocabulary:
- Interface
- Interaction
- User
- Software
- Hardware
- Considerations
- Constraints

Graphical User Interface (GUI)

A Graphical User Interface, known more commonly as a GUI, is a visual representation of an operating system that is presented to the user to make their interaction more meaningful. In almost all instances of modern operating systems, Android, iOS, MacOS and Windows a GUI is used. It includes graphical representations such as buttons, and icons. Interactions between the user and the computer are performed by clicking on these icons and buttons as opposed to text-based or command-based interactions discussed previously.

Revision pointers:

- Microsoft Windows is a commonly used example of a GUI
- Windows 10 is successful and easy to use because of its GUI
- The GUI helps the user understand the functionalities present within the computer through Graphical icons. A click on the icon initiates the action and the user's desired communication.
- Thus, GUI provides the functionality by abstracting the hard to understand each component/module's technical details and provides hassle-free usage of the system.

Advantages:

- Simple to use and usually has followed a evolution in design making users feel confident with new iterations of the software
- It is usually 'attractive' and 'intuitive' making people want to interact with the system
- Novice users with limited knowledge can use the computer and perform basic functions because of the GUI
- Searching the system in a GUI is easier than text-based interfaces or command line interfaces. It provides a visual representation of files present and provides details about it.
- All of the computers outputs and responses are visually displayed e.g. Task manger in Windows shows a graphical representation of the CPU and HDD/SDD usage.

Disadvantages:

- A user has limited features, in reality, for the average user this will not impact them, But because a GUI is restrictive, a user can often only do what has already been pre-programmes.
- A user cannot edit the basic functionality of a system.
- GUI's are power hungry. They take more CPU power than command line interfaces
- Outputs can be slow when compared to command-based Interfaces.
- GUI's are memory heavy. They take a large chunk of the computers primary and secondary memory capacities

Natural Language Interface

Natural-language user interfaces are often known as LUI or NLUI. They are a type of HCI where known language such as verbs, phases and clauses ace as user interfaces controls of the user. This language is used to create, select and modify data within software applications.

The key characteristic of LUI is their speed and ease of use. However, often LUI suffer from a break down in communication between the user and computer. LUI sometimes don't understand the users input due to the input not being clear (ambiguous) or the user having misspelt part of the command.

A search engine such as Google™ is an example of a LUI. The search engine finds targeted answers to the user's question or statement. Search engines focus on key words to return websites that meet the user's request. For example, when asked a question such as 'which English football team is the most successful?' the search engine will ignore the question and instead search for the keywords – English football team, successful, football team most successful. Often the information returned to the user will contain the answer to their query with the most relevant, and most likely to meet the users needs, being put at the top of the results list.

Modern NLUI include systems such as Siri, Google Home and Alexa. Whilst these may require a GUI in some cases to display results, they use a NLUI to allow the user to search using dictation.

Key Vocabulary:
- CPU
- Primary Storage
- Secondary Storage
- GUI
- LUI
- NLUI
- Dictation
- Telephony
- Wearable Tech
- Assistive Tech
- Embedded Systems

NLUI allows the user the following ways to interact with a computer system:

- Dictation – Speaking to devices such as Siri, Bixby, Google Home or Amazon Alexa
- Telephony – Voicemail systems that allow the user to interface with them using voice. An example of this might eb your bank who ask you to state, suing a few words, the reason for your call.
- Wearables – Apple Watch, Samsung Watch, Fitbits etc allow the user to interact with them using their voice
- Assistive technology – Many users with disabilities use NLUI to interact with their systems. Steven Hawkins, the famous scientist, used an NLUI and GUI combination to write over 16 books. Callers text to speech is a feature on many smart phones that read aloud the users phone information.
- Embedded Applications – Speech recognition in software such as WhatsApp allow the user to dictate their message. Most smart phones also now allow users to state a command such as 'call home' and then process and execute this accordingly.

Resources

The HCI is always going to be impacted by the resources used to access it and run it. You may have experienced this yourself when you have downloaded a new piece of software, operating system, or app and noticed that your device has significantly slowed down. You may have also experienced issues with your HCI's productivity through 'failing' peripheral devices such as mice, keyboards, speakers or even screen.

Display Screen

The screen that the user is viewing the HCI on will dramatically affect the experience for the user and the HCI's visuals. It is impossible to list all possibilities of screen types and their pros and cons as this is too complicated and has too many variables.

Below is a list of screen types for you to consider:

Screen Type	Key Characteristics	Pros	Cons
Touch screen - Smart Phone or Tablet	<ul><li>Usually, high resolution</li><li>Allows for input as well as display</li><li>Optimised for different settings - light and dark rooms</li><li>Has built in gesture commands</li></ul>	<ul><li>High resolution</li><li>Clear to see</li><li>Has input options</li><li>User can already use</li></ul>	<ul><li>Limited in size</li><li>Often has optimisation issues for Larger HCI designs</li><li>Always runs a GUI</li></ul>
Monitor - desktop	<ul><li>Vary in size from 17 inch to 49 inch</li><li>Variety of sizes and image quality available up to 4K</li><li>Some have touch screen interactivity</li><li>Project a GUI on a screen for user to interact with using a range of peripherals</li></ul>	<ul><li>Variety of sizes</li><li>Variety of prices to suit any budget</li><li>Image quality can be superior to any other display</li><li>Image settings can be managed easily</li><li>Allow for split/portioning</li><li>Multiple input options</li></ul>	<ul><li>Can be heavy</li><li>Can become 'outdated' quickly</li><li>Have fixed inputs</li><li>Can lead to health complaints if not adjusted/set up correctly</li><li>Some HCI's can be distorted on a larger screen</li></ul>
Monitor - Display	<ul><li>Can be scaled up to 300 inches</li><li>Automatically scale the input image</li><li>Some have touch screen functionality</li><li>Project a GUI to be seen by a wider audience</li><li>Suitable for displays</li></ul>	<ul><li>Variety of sizes</li><li>Variety of prices to suit any budget</li><li>Image quality can be superior to any other display</li><li>Image settings can be managed easily</li><li>Multiple input options</li></ul>	<ul><li>Can be heavy</li><li>Can be susceptible to damage</li><li>Have fixed inputs</li><li>Some HCI's can be distorted on a larger screen</li></ul>

Task:

Read the below information and suggest, and justify, a recommended display for each person.

Jon is the IT Manager at a large hospital based in Newcastle. New guidelines state that all wards must display information regarding the ward's current status, key members of staff and statistics. There are 45 wards, and each will require the information to be displayed above the nurse's station. As this has not medical benefit to the patients, Jon has been requested to keep the cost as low as possible whilst providing a clear message. Suggest and justify a display that Jon could purchase and install on each of the wards.

Pooja is a freelance photographer who covers weddings, baby shoots and animal portraits. She wishes to have a display that automatically displays the image she has just taken for her client to see. As the client and Pooja are in the same room, she doesn't feel this needs to be mounted to the wall. Suggest and justify a display that Pooja could purchase to accomplish her wish.

External peripherals

HCI's need interaction. No matter whether they are command line, menu based, GUI or natural language they all require peripherals to allow the user to engage and interact with them.

An example of peripherals that allow user input are listed in the table below:

Peripheral	Main utility	Which HCI uses this peripheral?	Cost
Keyboard	To allow the user to input text-based data into the system.	Command Line Interface (CLI) Graphical User Interface (GUI) Natural Language Interface	£
Mouse	To allow the user to interact with the system and to make selections	Menu Driven interface Graphical User Interface (GUI) Natural Language Interface	£
Microphone	To allow the user to input information into the system through voice/ speech	Graphical User Interface (GUI) Natural Language Interface	££
Graphical Tablet	To allow the user to input drawings into the system	Graphical User Interface (GUI)	£££

Assistive Technology for user interaction

There are many reasons why a user may use assistive technology. They may have a physical disability that prevents them from interacting with a HCI in the same way as able-bodied people, or they may have a barrier such as literacy or language that prevents them from using an HCI. Like the table above, below are a list of assistive technologies that allow user interactions with an HCI.

Task:

Complete the table:

Peripheral	Main utility	Which HCI uses this peripheral?	Cost
Puff Suck Switch		Menu Driven interface	
		Graphical User Interface (GUI)	
Speech to text		Menu Driven interface	
		Graphical User Interface (GUI)	
		Natural Language Interface	
Text to speech		Graphical User Interface (GUI)	
		Natural Language Interface	

Memory and Storage

Memory or storage is the collective term used to describe the components of the computer that store things. Different parts of the computer's memory are used for different storage like your long- and short-term memory.

Primary Storage

The primary storage in a computer system is the main memory that is used. It is a component, or a part, of the system that holds data, programs, information and instructions that are currently in use by the user.

Remember, a computer system doesn't necessarily mean a PC, a computer system could be a mobile, tablet, games console or an embedded system. All these computer systems require memory to function

All primary memory is stored on the motherboard itself. The location of primary memory is important because it means that the data it holds can be read and written extremely quickly. This allows the processor (CPU) to have the fastest possible access to the data and instructions which speeds up the system.

There are four main types of primary storage:

- Read only memory (ROM)
- Random access memory (RAM)
- Flash memory
- Cache memory

Two terms you must know are **volatile** and **non-volatile.** Volatile means that when the power is lost, the data is lost. Non-volatile in contrast means that even when the power is lost, the data isn't. In the systems primary storage ROM is non-volatile, which is important because the ROM holds the instructions to boot the system, this is called the boot sequence. RAM on the other hand is volatile and so all of its data is lost when it loses its electrical charge.

When compared to other forms of storage, notably secondary storage, primary storage is limited in its size. In the average modern computer, primary storage is around 4GB in size.

Task:

Answer the questions below

1. What does RAM stand for? (1)
2. What does ROM stand for? (1)
3. Explain the term volatile (3)
4. State the purpose of ROM in a computer system? (2)

RAM and ROM

Read only memory (ROM) is non-volatile primary storage. It keeps its contents when the computer is turned off.

As it states in its name, ROM can only be read by the computer and the user, and it cannot be written to. This means that ROM is ideal for storing instructions and data that are needed for the computer to run. The data it holds are pre-programmed into the system by the manufacturer and they cannot be changed. Think of ROM like the part of your brain that remembers for your heart to beat and you to breath. These instructions are pre-installed in you at the point of conception, they can't be changed or re-written to allow your heart to beat faster or to allow you to stop breathing, they can't be deleted or changed. ROM is the same.

The BIOS (Basic Input Output System) is housed in the ROM. The BIOS runs as soon as the computer is turned on. The BIOS checks that the hardware is all working as it should be and then loads the computers operating system.

Random access memory (RAM) is volatile. As soon as the computer system is switched off all its data is lost. It is called random access because the data that is housed within it can be stored and accessed from any location, The saving process is not logical.

The data that is stored within the RAM all relates to applications and processes currently in use. These could be applications such as Google Chrome © or an open document or even the operating system itself.

Unlike ROM, RAM can be written to and read from making it a read/write primary storage option. The contents of RAM can change at any time depending on the users' needs and requests, the interesting thing about RAM is that the more you have the faster your machine will be because it can hold more data and can run programs simultaneously. This ability makes it unique when compared to other primary storage.

Key Vocabulary:
- **Primary Storage**
- **Secondary Storage**
- **BIOS**
- **RAM**
- **ROM**
- **Read Only**
- **Read/Write**

Flash Memory

Flash memory is another form of storage. Like RAM it can be written to and overwritten. However, unlike RAM, which is volatile, flash memory is non-volatile, which as you now know, means that you can turn off the power and the data will not be lost.

Flash memory is fast to read and write too, but not as fast as RAM. It requires a small amount of power from the power supply unit (PSU) and it contains no moving parts meaning it is less prone to failure. It is the ideal storage solution for portable technology as when dropped, unlike a hard disk drive, because it is unlikely to damage.

Flash memory is now commonly, and widely, used in the form of SSD (Solid State Drives) and USB memory sticks.

Cache Memory

Cache memory is one of the harder types of primary storage for people to understand. It is a type of volatile RAM which is separate to the normal RAM and is built into the processor of the system.

Data can be transferred to and from the cache more quickly than from the RAM. This means that the CPU often uses the cache to temporarily hold data and instructions that the processor is likely to reuse. Due to its location, within the processor, it makes the transfer of data faster because the processor doesn't have to wat for the data to be fetched from the RAM as part of the fetch, decode, execute (FDE) cycle.

The higher storage capacity a computers cache has, the faster it will run/operate. The cost of cache memory is high because of its high-speed capabilities. The lower the capacity, the cheaper it is and therefore often computer systems have low sizes of cache memory built in.

There are two types of cache memory:

- L1 cache. This has a very fast data transfer rate but is very small in size. It is mainly used to hold the most frequently used instructions
- L2 cache. This is bigger than L1 but is slower. It is used to hold the data that is still used frequently by the processor but less frequently than that stored in L1 cache.

Task:

Complete the table:

Primary Storage	Key characteristics	Impact on HCI
ROM		
RAM		
Flash		
CACHE		

Secondary Storage

All secondary storage is non-volatile. Secondary storage is used as long-term storage, like your long-term memory. It is primarily used to store programs and data indefinitely. If a computer system didn't have secondary storage all the systems programs and data would be lost the moment the computer was turned off or lost power.

We have several different types of secondary storage, and each device has its own key characteristics. Every scenario in IT is different and because of this different device will be more suited to certain scenarios than others.

Below are the main forms of secondary storage used in modern computing:

- Hard Disk Drive
- Solid State Drive
- USB Memory Stick
- Magnetic Tape

Not all computers will need secondary storage. Embedded systems like your microwave or central heating system may not need to store data when it is switched off and so can operate perfectly well on RAM and ROM

Storage type	Characteristics	Pros	Cons	Cost
Hard Disk Drive (HDD)	• High capacity • Cost effective • Moving parts • Universally used	• Cheap • High capacity to cost ratio • Universal • Used for many years • Easy to install	• Not durable • Moving parts • Data recovery is difficult • Has a maximum read/write number	££
Solid State Drive (SSD)	• High Capacity • Flash memory • Quick read/write • No moving parts • Universal connections to motherboard	• Fast read/write • Easy to install • No moving parts • Extremely durable	• Expensive per Gb in comparison to HDD	£££
USB Memory Stick	• Portable • Flash memory • Varying storage capacities • No moving parts	• Cheap • USB – universal serial bus, universally used • Easy to use • No moving parts	• Not durable • Susceptible to damage • Easy to lose • Easy for data theft	£
Magnetic Tape	• High capacity • Cheap	• Can store a lot of data • Cheap per Gb when compared to other secondary storage	• Data stored sequentially • Specialist equipment needed to read data • Less durable	£

Processing Power

First, let's look at what this title means. Processing power is relating to the power the CPU, central processor, has and operates at. This is measured in MHz (megahertz) or gHz (gigahertz).

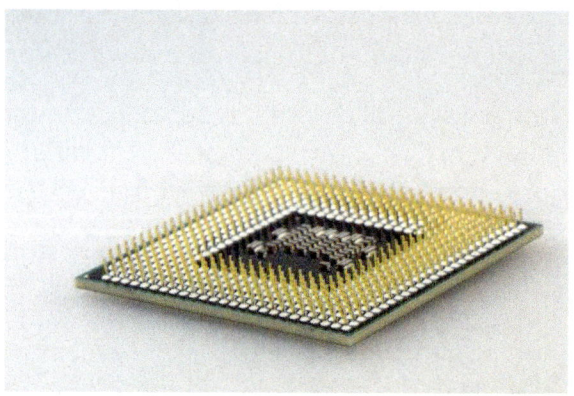

The speed of the CPU is known as the clock speed or the clock rate. This number indicates how fast the CPU can run. The speed is directly linked to the number of instructions that the CPU can deal with in a single second. A 3 gHz CPU will perform three billion cycles a second.

Typically, a computer has a maximum clock speed which is set by the manufacturer, similar to a car that is regulated to a maximum speed at the point of production. It is possible to change the speed of a CPU to make it run faster and this is known as overclocking. This isn't advised because often further components linked to the CPU struggle to match its new speed.

A HCI will require a certain clock speed to operate with CLI needing less processing power than a GUI. As GUI's develop and grow, they may require a faster processor to execute its instructions. This is the main reason why not all computers can run new software or operating systems or significantly slow down when these are installed.

System Requirements

All HCI's are provided to the consumer with a list of clear system requirements. These are the minimum system requirements when installing that piece of software. It is important for the success of the HCI that these are met entirely otherwise the user may experience inconsistences or issues with the HCI.

Upon its release in 2021, Microsoft Windows 11™ had its own set of clear system requirements. The system requirements took into consideration:

- The display type: *High definition (720p) display that is greater than 9" diagonally, 8 bits per colour channel.*
- The processor type: *1 gigahertz (GHz) or faster with 2 or more cores on a compatible 64-bit processor or System on a Chip (SoC).*
- The RAM: *4Gb*
- The storage *64Gb or larger storage device,*
- The graphics card: *Compatible with DirectX 12 or later with WDDM 2.0 driver.*

Data obtained from Microsoft website – Windows 11 Specifications

Software Considerations

Software can be broken down into operating system, application software and utility software. Each of these categories perform different duties within the computer system and will each have different HCI's that allow the user to interact with them.

Operating Systems

An operating system which is commonly known as an OS controls the overall operation of the computer system. Its HCI is fundamentally important because it allows the user to interact with the hardware (system) and with the application and utility software.

Common OS:

Windows, Apple macOS, Apple's iOS, Android, Chrome, Ubuntu, Linux, and Unix

The choice of operating system is often the user's choice and most systems allow any operating system to be loaded onto them. Historically, Apple™ products have been restricted to only using their own operating systems and likewise their operating systems, historically, have only worked on their devices. Games consoles run their own unique OS but in recent editions Microsoft Xbox© have ran a similar version to their Windows™ OS.

The operating system performs some very important tasks:

- **HCI** – it provides the end user with an interface that allows the user to interact with the computer system
- **Management** – it manages and oversees the
    - **CPU Management** – It checks that it is working correctly. It also manages applications and executes and cancels processes as and when needed
    - **Memory Management** – It transfers programs to and from the correct memory locations and allocates free space between programs
    - **Peripheral Management** – It opens, closes and writes to peripheral devices such as storage attached to the machine, printers, monitors and speakers
- **Multi-tasking** – it allows the user to use multiple applications at one time. This means the user can listen to Spotify™ whilst using Microsoft PowerPoint™
- **Organisation** – It creates a management system called a directory to store files and information in a logical way
- **Security** – It allows the user security when using a machine by allowing them to have user accounts and passwords
- **Utilities** – It provides tools for managing and organising the hardware.

Task:

Research. Working with a partner or as part of a group gather some images and information about the design of the HCI on the following operating systems:

Windows, Apple macOS, Apple's iOS, Android, Chrome, Ubuntu, Linux and Unix

Use the following questions to help you:

How does the user interact?

What does the menu look like?

How do icons appear?

Are there similarities with other OS's?

Digital Platforms

The HCI relates to the operating system but also to every application that the user interacts with. Different applications, or delivery method, may require a slightly different HCI design or implementation. A delivery method is the term used to describe the way in which the data is displayed to the user, e.g., a mobile app or a website.

Databases

Databases are used all over the world and in many different industries. You will have used a database and often not even realised. This is likely to be because a good database ah a good HCI that make the user confident to interact.

A database has many functions, options and instructions that may be running individually or simultaneously at any one time. There are two sides to a database, the back end and the front end. The back end is the development side, and this will have different HCI to the front end.

The back end of the database may allow the user to code their instructions, or to build features using advanced wizards. The front end should be clean and clear for the user to operate the system confidently and quickly. The HCI is dependent on:

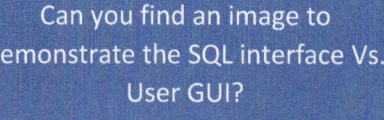

Can you find an image to demonstrate the SQL interface Vs. User GUI?

- The digital platforms purpose
- The users' needs and requirements for the system

The HCI for the developer is likely to be a combination of a CLI, menu driven interface and a GUI whereas the GUI for the user is likely to just be a GUI.

Mobile App

Who is a mobile app for? Its for current customer and returning customers not new customers. You wouldn't advertise a new customer only differ in an app for instance, because new customers wouldn't have it yet.

A company who uses an app must consider its HCI and its design. All apps run on a GUI and so the developer needs to have the following in their mind when developing the HCI.

- Is the app going to be clear and easy to use/navigate?
- Can the user access all the information on their devices?

The HCI needs to consider the power consumption and processing power of the user's device as well as the screen/display size. An app, or application, is likely to be used on a screen size of 7 inches or greater, therefore consideration and appreciation needs to be given by the developer to the users input. How big are the buttons and interaction points for the user?

Task:

Working with a partner or as part of a group discuss three applications you rate and don't rate.

Explain why you feel the way you do about the app and discuss the apps pros and cons. If possible, screenshot your applications HCI and then annotate it on the computer with areas of strength and weakness.

Use the following questions to help you:

How does the user interact?

What does the menu look like?

How do icons appear?

Spreadsheet

Unlike a database, a spreadsheet usually only has one HCI which both the developer and the user can see. However, the developer can apply restrictions through the HCI to remove access to certain cells, rows, columns, or sheets.

A spreadsheets HCI, although a GUI is a Menu Driven Interface for the most part with the user having a series of menus, they can use to access the spreadsheets controls and inner workings.

The HCI allows users to control formatting and display options to highlight cells and areas of interest, these modifications to the HCI aren't unique to spreadsheets but allow for personalisation of a pre-made HCI.

Websites Vs. Mobile Apps

Who is a website for? A website is to attract new customers, bring in new leads and to be a digital shopfront for a business. Since the start of the world wide web in the late 1990's websites have been on a journey. Hugely popular in the early 2000's with every company wanting to be online, website popularity died out at the dawn of the smart phone era between 2008 and 2011. At this time apps became far more superior and widely used with Apple™ coining the slogan 'there's an app for that'. But as applications grew, and users began to move away from these storage hungry digital artefacts and started moving back toward web browsing.

The reason for these transitions between apps and websites? The HCI of course. Early websites were built to be viewed on a display connected to a computer system, a display such as a screen or monitor. As the worlds connection to the world wide web went mobile, the display changed and shifted to a range of 7inch smart phones and 12inch tablets. This meant the HCI designs of the initial websites were no longer fit for purpose, they simply became unusable.

Remember:

The internet hasn't just always been around in the way that we know it. A lot has happened in the last 25 years!

The UK gets the Internet - 1998

WiFi Capabilities – 2001

Broadband rollout from 2001 – 2004

Fibre broadband – 2008

3G widely used in the UK – 2007

Early website HCI characteristics (1994-2010):

- Singular HCI for the website that needed to work on all display types and with all input types
- A horizontal menu bar across the top of the screen with links to pages
- Static images of content corresponding to text place holders
- Text – lots of text. Descriptions, wording, and information being displayed to the user on their screen was mainly in a text format.
- Un-optimised web pages that were unable to scale to different sized screens
- Text based hyperlinks

Later website HCI characteristics (2010-present day):

- A separate HCI for mobile devices such as smart phones and for PCs with bigger displays.
- A separate HCI for different input methods e.g., touch screen or mouse
- A menu that appeared in a collapsed state often signified globally as three lines
- Images and videos that can be played on different devices and with different connections
- Limited text on the screen and the ability to embed documents into code
- Optimised web pages that read the metadata of a device to identify connection and display to provide the user with the best HCI
- GUI based buttons as links allowing multiple inputs

Task:

Using the website archive.org/web search and document the progression of five globally used websites over time. Take a screenshot of each iteration and then write a report on the evolution of that website, its positives and negative.

User interaction methods

In the table below you will be able to see a list of user interaction methods and their advantages and disadvantages. You will need to know this information for your exam.

User Interaction method	Explanation	Advantage	Disadvantage
Gesture	Gesture control allows the user to control a device without making any contact with it. An example of this you might have experienced is when you swipe your hand over a modern android device it takes a screenshot? Or when you swipe your hand over an iPhone it turns on or when you pick up your smart phone and it turns on and looks for a face to recognise. These gestures allow the user to use their device without needing to know any set commands, button presses of procedures. **Only can be used with a GUI.**	• Doesn't rely on a user's literacy skills to have to read an instruction. • Allows for easy navigation e.g. turning a page on a Kindle. • Allows the user to use common gestures to interact with technology	• Gestures must be known in advance • Can accidentally trigger an instruction to the HCI without meaning to • Can be 'intermittent' • The user does not know if the gesture has been registered unless the action is performed
Keyboard	Allows a user to interact with a HCI by typing in information. The keyboard can have pre-set keys for certain actions such as copy and paste or a play button for a song. The keyboard also allows the user to use applications and type in content as they wish. **Can be used with CLI, Menu Driven Interface and GUI**	• Easy to use and often in a standard QWERTY layout • Buttons are clear to the user • Allows the user to control and edit	• Various layouts • Language dependent • Button presses need to be known in advance • User can make mistakes
Mouse	It's the user's pointer, the users finger. It allows the user to interact with the HCI by clicking on a series of **W**indows **I**cons and **M**enus using the mouse which is their **P**ointer. **Can be used with a Menu Driven interface or a GUI**	• Easy to use and often in a standard layout • Limited button commands • Allows the user to control and edit	• More complex mice are available •
Touch	A touch screen incorporates an onscreen keyboard, and their finger is their pointer/mouse. **Can be used with a Menu Driven interface or a GUI**	• Easy to use • Often button commands • Allows the user to control and edit with their digits	• Difficult for users with accessibility issues • If a screen is smashed it can impact the touch element
Voice	Voice allows the user to interact with the HCI by speaking to it. Like Google Home, Amazon Alexa, and Siri. It makes interactions with the system quicker than typing. **Can be used with a Natural Language Interface or a GUI**	• Easy to use • Allows the user to control with their voice • Understands various languages and accents • Can how images and video as well as sound	• Can misunderstand people • Microphone always being on can lead to privacy concerns • The user needs to be in the vicinity of the microphone •

Chapter 3: Data and testing

Information Vs Data

Data is made up of raw facts and figures. Most importantly data has no meaning at all.

An example of data might be **01293.** Now, alone this is a series of numbers joined together in what we call a string. It is in fact the area code at the start of a telephone number for numbers in the Crawley area of West Sussex.

Area codes can be 3, 4, or 5 digits long and alone have no meaning. Until you give them **context.** When given context these area codes come more meaningful, and it is at this point they become **information**.

Digit length	Explanation	Example
3	3-digit codes all start with 02, followed by a further 8 digit phone numbers, and serve larger metropolitan area populations	020 London numbers 023 Southampton & Portsmouth 024 Coventry 028 Northern Ireland 029 Cardiff
4	4-digit codes, starting with either 011x or 01×1 and followed by a further 7-digit phone numbers serve large cities and surrounding areas.	0113 Leeds 0114 Sheffield 0151 Liverpool 0161 Manchester 0191 Tyneside
5	5 Digit Codes are used for the remaining codes and begin with 01 and are 5 digits long, then followed by a 5 or 6-digit phone number. Most UK landline numbers are a total of 11 digits, however some locations still have a mixture 10 digits and 11. Matlock 01629 has several 10 digit numbers, as does Buxton 01298. Over 580 areas now use this format.	01977 Castleford 01246 Chesterfield 01765 Ripon 01942 Wigan 01204 Bolton 01293 Crawley 01403 Horsham

So information is data with context, we can use the following formular to convert Data into information:

Information - Data + Meaning + Context

Task:

Provide some context to the following data:

1. Postcode – RH6 0NP
2. Car Registration plate – PR07 8LP
3. Flight numbers – BA1442

Using data in the real world

Data is rapidly becoming the currency of success. Businesses need data to pursue leads, customers, and materials. However, the need is not for any data, the need is for good, high-quality data that has been collected and managed well.

Data Types

When data is harvested (collected) it needs to be organised in a logical way. We use data types to help organise the data and identify it easily.

Below is a list of data types, their characteristics and uses:

Data Type		Context and Characteristics	Examples
Alphanumeric		Alphanumeric is a combination of letters and numbers. It could be used to represent an ID, post code or any piece of data where both letters and numbers are connected as one string	AD1 RH6 9AQ Susan1
Boolean		This is where there are only two options presents to the end user. It is good when asking the user, a set question where they can only have one of two responses	Yes/No Black/White I/O
Date		Little explanation required here. This is a data that refers to a date being inputted but the user. **Note:** Different countries have different formats for their dates	17/02/2021 2021/02/17 02/17/2021
Numeric	Currency	This data type will be sued for any data related to currency. That doesn't have to be pound sterling, it could be dollars, euros or any world currency including crypto currency	£4.50 $7.80 €5.90
	Decimal	This should be used for any number that has a **fixed** position point or decimal point. A number that has a decimal after it, denoting a fraction of a further number	78.60 95.67 51.5
	Integer	The integer data type is used for whole numbers without a decimal point.	5 55 87
	Percentage	The percentage data type is used for any number that represents a percentage. This is often as a result of a calculation.	65% 87%
	Real	Similar to a decimal data type a real data type is used for any number that has a **floating** decimal point. This should be used for changeable data dependent on the users input	151.68 1.69 2369.68
Text		This relates to any data that is 'plain text', a chunk/block of text. It may have numbers in it, or special characters. **Note:** Text needs to be used as a data type when using a phone number if it starts with 0	Any part of this book

Validation and Verification

Data validation is a process that the systems user/designer can undergo to ensure that the data entered is of a good quality. There are three forms of validation, validation rules, validation constraints or check routines. These check for correctness, meaningfulness and that the security of the data that has been inputted into the system. Verification is the process of checking the data meets the requirements of the user.

Data Validation Tools

Tool Name	Tool Purpose	How does this stop data errors?
Format check	Format checks are performed on the date, check digit, time, currency code, and country code fields. For date fields, the format check verifies that the date provided is valid.	By checking the data that has been entered meets the formatting expected there is less of a chance that the data is inaccurate or of poor quality.
Input mask	This form of validation checks that the user has made an input into the field that meets a preassigned combination. The data might check for certain type of data or string of data such as letters or numbers.	This ensures that the data that is expected is entered and that there are no mistakes. Input masks might be used for a post code or a telephone number and pre-set what is expected from the user
Length check	This check looks at the length of the users input to check it is of sufficient length. This ensures that there aren't too many characters entered or that the right number of characters are entered. This might be used for a mobile phone number.	This can be used to ensure that the data is of a length suitable for the question. It can be used on any data but commonly used on names where it is unlikely for them to exceed 20 letters. So, a length check is used to prevent a person entering random data that is too long.
Limited choice	This provides the user with a set number of choices. This might be used for colour selection, or an item selection from a set number of buttons.	This is good when there are between 2 and 5 options for the users to select from. It limits their choice and makes the data more accurate
Drop down list	As the name suggests, this is a list of options which the user can select from a drop-down list.	Brilliant for a selection that has to be from a pre-determine list. An example might be counties in the UK.
Radio buttons	These little circular buttons which fill with a black dot when selected provide a simple user selection. Often these are used for yes/no or male/female options.	Used often for options that have 1, 2 or 3 possible selections. A user selecting Male or Female has reduced chances of mistake than typing.
Tick list	As the name suggests this is a list of options where the user has ticked an option.	Good for selection to indicate the choice of a user. Again, reducing the risk of error and the risk of a large array of options being given.
Lookup	This looks up values in a table based on set criteria entered by the user.	This can be used to ensure consistency and that the correct data is entered e.g. there are only seven possible days of the week
Presence check	This checks the user has made an input and prevents a field being left blank. Have you ever seen a red message appear when you forget to fill in a box on a form?	Simply checks that some data entry has been made. Often when there is missing data a red message will appear with a * indicating such error.
Range check	Checks that a value falls within the specified range	When the answer must fall in a range the range check ensures that this is the case.

Data Collection Methods

Data collection methods can be split into two categories. Primary collection and secondary collection. Primary data collection means it has been done by you or the organisation you work for. Secondary collection methods are those where whereby the company pays an external company for their data or use data that is in the public domain.

> Did you know that primary and secondary are both terms used in other subjects such as History, geography and English. They all mean the same thing!

Primary Data Collection Methods

- Email
- Interview
- Questionnaire or Survey - Online of in person
- Consumer Panel

Secondary Data Collection Methods

- Books
- Government Statistics (Office of National Statistics)
- Magazines
- Websites
- Social Media
- TV/Radio or Online Video

Task:

For each of the data collection methods above explain what data could be collected from this method. Why this method would be successful for the collection of data and potential negatives of using this method.

Page | 38

Chapter 4: Storage

Computer storage acts like the memory of a human. It is used to store data, information, instructions and software. There are different forms of computer storage, they each have benefits and negatives. You need to be able to explain the characteristics of each device and be able to explain the advantages and disadvantages of the devices. Like with other areas of IT, these devices are split into logical and physical categories. Logical devices are those that we can not see or touch, like cloud storage. Physical devices are those that we can see, and we can touch and examples of these are hard drives, solid state drives and optical media.

Logical Storage Devices

An example of logical storage is cloud. The cloud has been a term used since around 2007 when companies started offering virtual storage facilities to paying customers. Cloud storage is excellent for anyone with a strong internet connection. It allows users access to their files remotely meaning wherever they are, whenever they want, they can access their files. This is opposed to the files being in a fixed location. However, not everyone has internet connection and mobile connections are variable across the planet meaning that whilst, theoretically, users can access their files anywhere and at any time, this is only possible with a connection.

Task:

It is a common misconception that the cloud is in the sky. You can understand why, the name suggests so, however this isn't the case.

1. Explain the term, the cloud, to a person who knows nothing about it. Include an explanation of where the storage is and why the user needs an internet connection.
2. Find four cloud storage providers. How much do they charge for their services? Do they have any information about what can be stored on their cloud platform?

Physical Storage Devices

The bracket of physical storage can be split further into the two categories of internal and external physical storage. This description refers to the location of the device, wither inside of the machine or outside of the machine, connected possibly via a USB.

Internal Physical Storage

Primary Hard Drive - this is the computers main form of storage. It will be higher in capacity and could be in the form of a Hard Disk Drive or Solid-State Drive. This device will house the computers operating system, software, drivers and files.

Network Drive -The network drive is a fixed location within a network where items can be stored for the users of that network. Network drives are useful for sharing files, software and peripherals.

External Physical Storage

Portable external hard disk drive (HDD) - This is an HDD that is attached to a PC usually via USB to allow file and data transfer. They are good to move data, but they do run the risk of failure as the HDD inside has moving parts. Due to the continued movement, unplugging and plugging in of the device, it is recommended that the devices are always backed up and not used to store a lot of data.

Portable external solid-state drive (SSD) - Unlike its portable HDD counterpart, the SSD doesn't have moving parts and can cope better with continued movement, accidental dropping and the continued unplugging/plugging in to a computer. It is faster than the HDD but is more expensive comparatively per GB of storage than the HDD.

Network Attached Storage (NAS) - A series of HDD's or SSD's that are connected to a network or the internet. They allow file sharing and remote access and are good when used in conjunction with other applications for centralised management of a network. They are expensive and users must make sure that they are using NAS HDD and not a standard HDD as they are built differently.

Portable USB Flash Drives - Also known as thumb sticks/USB Memory Sticks - These are excellent for quick file transfer, and ease of use. However, easily lost, or broken, they are not advised for use with sensitive data or data that has not been backed up.

Wireless Network Drives - These drives, predominantly used for media sharing allow multiple users to stream their content wirelessly. The device, powered by a mains cable and connected to a small integrated network interface card, allow users to put files on them and then stream these files from a device remotely.

Chapter 5: Application of testing to a range of contexts

Importance and purpose of testing

Testing is vital to the success of any IT project. When we test, we ensure two things:

1. That the product (deliverable) works
2. That the product (deliverable) meets the requirements

Testing is done in two ways, formative and summative. Formative assessment is done throughout the creation of the product. This testing is done to inform the production process. Often, formative testing can go un-noticed, checking a button works when it's been made, checking the colour scheme matches the brief. However, some formative testing can be completed through continued phase reviews. Phase reviews happen at planned milestones within an IT project and are conducted to ensure that the phase meets the requirements. It is an opportunity for the IT specialist to manage a project and prevent it from going off track.

Summative testing is done at the end of the project, it takes into consideration the projects success by looking at the percentage of the success criteria that has been met. In this testing the specialist will look at their phase testing/reviews and use these to inform their final testing. Often, an outcome of summative testing is a percentage completion of the project, with the aim always to 100% meet all the clients' requirements and needs.

Test Data

Test data can be split into three categories, extreme, invalid (also known as erroneous) and valid. Below is a table explaining these types of test data:

Type of test data	What type of test data is this?	What role does this testing play?
Extreme	This is data that is at the upper and lower limits of the expectations	Tests the system to see how it will 'cope' with the minimum expected data and the maximum expected data.
Invalid (Erroneous)	This is data that is not expected in the field that it is entered.	It is used to check for validation and verification and to ensure that invalid data cant be entered accidentally.
Valid	A standard test, this checks the outcome of valid data being entered	Used to check that it is allowed and processed.

Types of testing

In software engineering and computer science, there are two types of testing that are performed by different people/users. Technical testing is testing undertaken by a technical user of the developer. This testing tests beyond the HCI. User testing is testing undertaken by a standard user and usually focusses on the functions of the system and the HCI.

Potential Testing

There are a variety of different tests that can be carried out to ensure the product is fit for market/use. Some of these are listed below:

Unit Testing
Unit testing is a technical test and focusses on the smallest unit of the software design. The unit test is used to test a specific element of the software only. This technical test is often conducted by a programmer as they build the code. An example test would be the programmer checking a button work as it should.

Integration Testing
Integration testing builds on unit testing by taking the unit tested elements and building a bigger section to be tested. An example, working with the button analogy, would be unit testing a series of buttons to allow integration testing of a menu system.

Regression Testing
Software is built in modules and stages. Regression testing believes that unit and integration testing has occurred and then checks that combined modules work as they should once combined. In a school, there will be a module for teachers, one for students and one for rooms. Independently these are all working and allow additions, redactions and edits. Regression testing tests that there are working links between these modules once combined.

Alpha Testing
This is the final technical test; this test is done internally within the team of developers. They imitate the user and check that everything they expect to work, works as it should.

Did you know?

You can sign up to be a beta tester and receive early releases of games and software.

Beta Testing
The first user test, beta testing is completed by the user/customer. It is conducted after release on the machines of the user and in a real-life environment. Beta testing is done with most video games, and software.

Stress Testing
The user and technical stress testing give unfavourable, unlikely, conditions to the software to see how it would perform. Examples might be multiple users, different machine specifications or continued invalid data testing.

Chapter 6: Cyber-security and legislation

Networks operate on the principles of communication and sharing. Unfortunately, these principles mean that network traffic and data risk being accessed by people who have no authority to do so (ie hackers).

A network attack is an attempt to gain access to, steal, modify or delete data on a network. Such attacks take several forms:

- Active - where the hacker attempts to modify or delete data, or to prevent a network from operating correctly. An example of this is denial of service (DOS) attacks on the internet, which use many internet-enabled computers to force a web server offline.
- Eavesdropping (passive) - where the hacker monitors a network in order to gain information. An example of this is wiretapping, where communications are monitored.
- External - where someone outside of an organisation attempts to hack its network.
- Internal - where someone within an organisation attempts to hack its network.

The number of network attacks in the world are growing daily.

Task:

Attacks happen every day, all over the world. However, on some occasions, they make the national news and affect millions of people.

Once such attack was the WannaCry attack in 2017. Do some research, using the internet, into the WannaCry attack and answer the following questions.

- What type of attack was this?
- What was the aim of the attack?
- What was the impact of the attack?
- How could it have been prevented?
- How was it stopped?

Hacking

Hacking is a term that is used far too widely. Very often, when someone says that they have been hacked, they haven't. Instead, they have been subject to a cyber security attack in the form of a virus or social engineering technique.

There are three types of hackers:

1. Black Hat
2. Grey Hat
3. White Hat

A very common misconception is that all hackers aim to cause damage or disruption, and that they all leave secretive lives or act in the name of cyber terrorism.

The truth in fact, is that hackers have existed for as long as electronic communication has. Alan Turing, the father of computer science, was a hacker. He worked to intercept ciphered messages coming from the Nazi empire. Yet when we consider a hacker, rarely do we envisage Alan Turing.

Black Hat Hacking

So, what is a black hat hacker? Well, a black hat hacker is the type of hacker you imagine. They are hackers who violate company security protocols for their own personal gain/profit or out of malice with the intension to cause mass disruption to the company's operation.

Black hat hackers are a global problem. The challenge for global law enforcement and governments are that these hackers often don't leave a trace and leave no evidence like a traditional crime scene. Black hat hackers often sue the computers of their victims across multiple jurisdictions. Whilst some authorities have been successful in shutting down sections of sites in one country, these hackers often have multiple nodes in different countries allowing the start-up of the hacking again and to allow them to operate 24/7 over different time zones.

Grey Hat Hacking

So, what is a grey hat hacker? Well unlike a black hat hacker a grey hat hacker is a computer scientist who often evades the law or typical ethical standards, but they do not do it with malicious intent but for their own satisfaction or enjoyment.

Grey hat hackers fall between black and white hat hackers. Unlike certified ethical hackers, grey hat hackers are still operating illegally.

Usually, grey hat hackers act in the public interest, if in their hacking pursuits they identify company weaknesses or loopholes they will often point them out to the company. The company often works alongside the hacker to fix the identified issue and often this leads to a reward for the grey hat hacker for identifying an issue. The difference between white and grey hat hacker is that a grey hat hacker isn't employed by the company and thus isn't bound contractually to fix the identified issues. Instead, should the company choose to ignore the hacker they can exploit the issue themselves or leak the issue online for other, potential black hat hackers to exploit.

White Hat Hacking

A white hat hacker has good intentions. they have the skill sets of black hat hackers, but they are employed by a company to test the system consistently and systematically for vulnerabilities. They therefore do not look to exploit a business for personal gain.

The purpose of the white hat hacker is to find the issue, fix the issue and save the company money in lost revenue, or fines.

A white hat hacker has the required knowledge to exploit software, networks or systems, but choose instead to work with the owner rather than against the, . These hackers are often labelled as cyber security analysts or experts.

Task:

There are several prevention methods that the user can take to prevent a black hat hacker gaining access to their machine/device. In your portfolio create a page called prevention methods. For each of the below explain the term, find an image and explain how this will act as a prevention to unauthorised access:

- Firewall
- Antivirus Software
- Antispyware software
- Operating System updates
- Only visiting reputable sites and downloading from secure sites

Social engineering

Social engineering is manipulating people into handing over confidential information such as a PIN or password. There are several forms:

Baiting

Much like catching a fish with bait, baiting is where a scammer uses a false promise or mistruth to capture the victim's attention and engagement. They do this to trap the user and then exploit them to steal their personal or financial information. In some instances, baiting is used to infect a computer with malware after capturing the users' personal credentials.

Phishing

This is where the scammer sends fraudulent communications such as emails that appear to originate from a reputable source. The clear goal with phishing is to steal sensitive data such as credit card details, credentials or to install malware on the victim's machine.

Pretexting

Pretexting can often, incorrectly, be known as cold calling. Pretexting happens when a situation or a pretext is created by the attacker in order to get the person to disclose their sensitive information. The information provided by the person can lead to monetary gain for the attacker or to the installation of malware on their machine. The information provided often wouldn't have been done so willingly outside the pretext and so the user is unaware they have been scammed.

An example of this is receiving a call from your bank, or not as the case may be, and them asking you a variety of questions to get through clearance. In fact, all you are doing is providing them with the information for them to clear your security clearance.

Quid pro quo

The hacker will offer a service or benefit in exchange for the information or access. The most common quid pro quo attack occurs when a hacker impersonates an IT team member from a large organisation.

Another example would be receiving a call from your internet service provider pretending to support you. For them to do this they need to access you details and account and so you provide them with the information.

Scareware

Scareware is a type of malware attack that claims to have found a virus on the computer or device. It gives the user the option to remove the found virus by clicking on a displayed button. This redirects the user to a download area where they download or buy malware to their machines.

Scareware acts as a gateway to more cyber security attacks. It 'scares' the user into irrational actions. Most people have Antivirus installed already, but in the moment panic and download from a non-reputable source.

Shoulder Surfing

The name suggests how this cyber security attack works. This is the situation where an unsuspecting user is being watched/monitored from a distance. The attacker is close enough to see the screen or keystrokes and then obtain personal information. It is one of the few social engineering attacks where the attacker must be close to the victim.

Malware

Malware is an umbrella term for a collection of 'malicious software' that has the intent to disrupt a machines functionality. This can be for financial gain, but often is for no other reason than to cause destruction to a machine.

The malware you are required to know are:

Adware	Adware is software that automatically displays or downloads advertising material such as banners or pop ups when a user is online.
Spyware	Spyware is software that is designed to enter your device, gather data about you and forward it on to a third-party without your consent. It uses technology such as key logs to log the keystrokes you make and monitor for consistent messages.
Botnet	A botnet is a number of internets connected devices. The botnet is controlled by a bot master, who controls the devices remotely. Botnets can be used to conduct Distributed Denial of Service Attacks, steal data, send spam, and allow the hacker to directly access the device and its connections. The bot master controls the bot net that they have created using command and control software.
Virus	A virus is a malicious piece of software often downloaded by the user onto the computer. Similar to a virus that humans get, a computer virus slows the computer down, makes certain function perform differently and can cause the computer to 'die' or fail to boot.
Worm	A worm, like its invertebrate counterpart, digs through the computer's hard drive and memory looking for key elements predetermined by the creator of the worm itself. It can replicate itself quickly and then can spread across a computer or network. As it spreads, a worm takes large amounts of bandwidth from the PC, overwhelming the system and making it unusable. Worms can also change files and delete them as they replicate.
Ransomware	Ransomware like its name suggests, holds a user's computer ransom. It is a malicious software that employs encryption techniques to encrypt the victims' computers information and files and then hold them ransom. Often, failure to pay the ransom amount results in the data being destroyed or shared online.
Trojan Horse	Arguably the most famous of viruses the trojan horse is a malicious code or software that looks legitimate to the user but allows an external person to take control of your computer. Named after the famous trojan horse used by the Greeks to penetrate Troy, this malicious software is designed to damage, disrupt, steal, or general impact a network negatively. The trojan becomes active when clicked by the user. Otherwise, it stays dormant.

Cyber Security Impacts

The impacts of cybercrime can be catastrophic. Any of the social engineering attacks or malware attacks could be used to cause data destruction, manipulation, modification, or theft. The impact of a DoS can have widespread ramifications for a business as their users are unable to access the devices and then complete their work.

Name	Impact	Possible outcomes
Data destruction	Data destruction aims to render the information irretrievable. Data destruction is used to ensure that any future users of the technology are unable to access any legacy data	<ul><li>Data being lost</li><li>Data being destroyed</li><li>A victim not receiving information that they should</li></ul>
Data manipulation	Can lead to misinformation being used within businesses. Can lead to fraud, where the victim is the person impacted. Data manipulation is where data is changed in some way.	<ul><li>Data that has been changed</li><li>Inaccurate data</li><li>Primary data becoming secondary data</li></ul>
Data modification	The attack alters the companies' assets of digital systems which can cause disruption to their operations. The system may not know it is happening unlike a DoS attack.	<ul><li>Data inaccuracies</li><li>Client/customer dissatisfaction</li></ul>
Data theft	Impacts for the victims and business. Business must report to the ICO for a breach of GDPR. Could lead to illegal activity with the data stolen.	<ul><li>Data could be sold</li><li>Data could be used illegally</li><li>Could lead to the distribution of malware</li></ul>
Denial of Service (DoS)	Prevents access to a device or devices. If this is a DoS attack on a server or NAS, the company could become impacted financially from the down time in their systems. Depending on the company's sector, clients may be impacted.	<ul><li>No access to systems</li><li>Reduced access to computer systems or services</li><li>'Down time' which impacts the customers</li></ul>
Identity Theft	Identity theft, where a person's details and identity is stolen. This can cause huge financial ramifications as well as legal implications for the victim.	<ul><li>Financial disturbance</li><li>Criminal records for the victim</li></ul>

Preventing Threats

One of the roles of the network manager is to ensure the network is safe from attacks and threats of any kind. There are many techniques that can be used to help keep a network safe. These can be broken down into three topics, physical prevention, logical prevention and the secure destruction of data.

Physical Protection Methods

Physical prevention methods are those which a person can physically touch or see. They are there to be used in an interactive way by the user.

Biometric Devices

Biometric devices include fingerprint scanners, iris scanners, and face recognition. A human's biometrics are unique to them making this form of prevention method strong and harder to crack. Usually, the hacker will require the physical presence of the victim to gain access through biometrics.

Image: Fingerprint scanners are a form of biometric security

Keypads

Keypads require user input for the user to proceed. Keypads might be seen on doors or safes and require a keycode from the user to progress. They can be used in conjunction with tiered levels of access to allow different users into different areas using differing codes.

Radio-frequency identification (RFID)

Is a form of wireless communication that uses electromagnetic or electrostatic signals to uniquely identify the user. They can be used as a card, a tag or as a chip. When used as a physical prevention method an RFID chip identifies the object and communicates with a lock. This can be coded to allow users access to certain rooms, to record who has accessed which room when and can also be controlled centrally to lock all doors in the case of an emergency.

Image: RFID Key Card often used in businesses for door locks

Dual Prevention Methods - Both logical and Physical

Firewalls

Named after a burning wall which is impassable, the firewall in a computer scans packets for malicious code or attack vectors. Should a packet of data be flagged as a potential threat the firewall stops it and prevents it from entering the device and network, essentially burning it up before it gets to cause damage. In large organisation the firewall is a separate piece of hardware making this both a physical and logical prevention method.

Secure Backups

Secure backups allow the user to securely back up their system at regular intervals. This means in the form of an attack, particularly ransomware, worm or virus, the system can be wiped and rebuilt from a previous point. Put simply it is a copy or archive of information on the device that can be called upon or restored if needed. Due to the need for an addition storage area, that is stored away from the primary device, secure backups are both logical and physical prevention methods.

Logical Prevention Methods

Logical prevention methods are those which a person can NOT physically touch or see. They are digital.

Access rights and permissions

An organisation can prevent cyber security attacks by having appropriate access rights and permissions for their users. Different access rights can be assigned to different users. This is called tiered levels of access. Where one user can access a certain set of a files and a separate user can access the same and more. This can mitigate cyber security attacks because it means that should a user's access be compromised they aren't able to access the entire system.

Anti-virus and Anti-Malware

The biggest prevention to so many of the attack's computers face is a reputable and up to date anti-virus or anti-malware software. This software can routinely scan for viruses and malware, locating them and putting them into 'quarantine'. The software can remove this form the device and act as a method of mitigation against most viruses and malware threats. Even social engineering attacks that lead to viruses entering a device will be detected. Social engineering attacks where the user provides the information are not protected by this software.

Two Factor Authentication (2FA)

This is a form of prevention that you will have likely used. It is used to access certain websites or services; it requires two forms of ID to access the system. For instance, when you have logged into Instagram and then need to input a code sent via txt to your device to authenticate that you are the person you say you are. it mitigates the risk of attack by making sure that the user is who they say that they are, the likelihood of the attacker having the credentials plus device is far less than them having just the credentials.

Encryption
Encryption takes the data and turns it into a cypher. This is cypher can only be turned back to plain text with the key. This is excellent to mitigate the risk of the data being intercepted during transmission to another machine. The attacker may obtain some data in the security attacker, but it is un-readable without the key to turn it back into plain text.

Usernames and Passwords
Our first form of defence and barrier to cyber security attacks is a strong password. The term strong password has become well known with many businesses and services now demanding that the user have a password that contains letters, numbers and special characters. This creates the combination required to gain entry infinitely harder to crack than just a password that contains letters.

Secure Destruction of Data
One way to prevent data from being accessed in a cyber security attack it to destroy it when it is no longer required. There are several ways that this can be done, erasing, sanitation, magnetic wipe, physical destruction.

Data erasure
This is a software based method of overwriting the data that is on a hard disk drive. The aim of this is to destroy all the electronic data on the device by re-writing the disk and saving into new sectors within the disk platters. This method of prevention ensures that no data is left on a hard drive when the hard drive is no longer needed or used. removing the data when it isn't used is key to the data not being accidentally accessed or stolen.

Data Sanitisation
This involves the secure and permanent erasing of sensitive data from the disk. This method guarantees that no residual data can be found even if a person were to try and complete intensive forensic analysis. This is again a mitigation that prevents an attack whereby an attacker finds a device or obtains a device and retrieves data from it.

Magnetic Wipe
Hard drives use magnetic residue to store their data like cassettes and tapes. A magnetic wipe is used to ensure that no magnetic residue is present on the disk. In some instances, after forensic analysis, previous magnetic residue can be read, and the data retrieved. A magnetic wipe will remove all data, including previously stored data and the drives various sectors.

Physical Destruction
This is by far the most selected answers for exam questions. Physical destruction is a method used to destroy a hard disk drive completely. By doing this the data is destroyed. Methods include, shredding, burning, and smashing. It is deemed a success when the hard drive is so damaged that no data can be used or retrieved.

> Because a HDD uses magnetic material to record data, even when deleted some data can be found. These methods prevent this from happening.

Legislation

Legislation is a term used to describe the laws to which all citizens of the UK must adhere to. The UK legislation which relates to Computer Science and IT include:

- Computer Misuse Act
- GDPR or General Data Protection Regulation Act
- Copyright, Designs and Patents Act
- Freedom of Information Act
- Health & Safety at Work Act
- Regulation of Investigatory Powers Act (RIPA)

Computer Misuse Act 1990

You would be mistaken for thinking that the Computer Misuse Act is the most relevant act when it comes to computer science, IT and the use of computers. However, written in 1990 this act does paint a vague picture of computer usage and it is widely argued that it is no longer fit for purpose.

The aim of the Computer Misuse Act is to protect all the personal data held by an organisation from unauthorised access and modification. When thinking about unauthorised access, we need to consider entering a computer system without permission. This is hacking, no matter the hat.

The three key offences are:

1. unauthorised access to computer material.
2. unauthorised access with intent to commit or facilitate commission of further offences.
3. unauthorised acts with intent to impair, or with recklessness as to impairing, operation of computer, etcetera.

Mitigating against Computer Misuse Act breaches/attacks:

A user can do several things to mitigate against the chance of being a victim of cybercrime and breach of the CMA. Below are some mitigations:

1. Never leave a device unlocked
2. Always ensure that the devices passwords are robust
3. Passwords protect files and documentation
4. Consider encryption for important and sensitive files

Task:

Can you explain the principles of the Computer Misuse Act to business? Explain how to mitigate against breaches of the act and procedures clients, customers and employees can take to avoid being subjected to an attack.

This guide could include the ways to make a 'strong' password, or the ways to password protect standard files within Microsoft Office.

GDPR 2016

GDPR, the general data protection regulation, was written into law in 2016 and it replaced the Data Protection Act.

It is a legal framework in European Union law that protects data and privacy in the European Union and European Economic Area. Despite leaving the EU, the UK still adheres to GDPR.

It is designed to support, protect and enable people and business to be in control of their data and the data held by companies about them.

Key principles to remember

The seven key principles to remember are:

- Lawfulness, fairness and transparency.
- Purpose limitation.
- Data minimisation.
- Accuracy.
- Storage limitation.
- Integrity and confidentiality (security)
- Accountability.

Being GDPR compliant:
- All business must have a designated GDPR lead knows as the Data Protection Officer. This person oversees the businesses data, processes and compliance.
- All data must be collected in a lawful way with the intentions of the data collection outlined from the start to the subject
- The purpose of data collection must be clear. Once collected the data can be only used for this purpose and not be used for other purposes to the advantage of the company. For example, a company may ask for information form customers about a product. They can't, unless the customer is notified, used this information for other purposes.
- Only required data must be collected. This means that if the subjects address bares no purpose to the company, they cannot make the entry of this information mandatory.
- The data must be kept up to date with the subject being asked at regular intervals whether any data has changed
- Storage and security of the data must be considered and upheld. The subject has provided the company with data and expect it to be stored securely and in a way that is not likely to be the subject of a cyber security attack of any kind.

Did you know?

GDPR is not impacted by Brexit? Despite leaving the EU, the UK still works with its counterparts in the EU on matters such as GDPR.

Copyright, Designs and Patents Act 1988

The Copyright Designs and Patents Act was written by the UK government to protect individuals' intellectual property and creations. When a person creates something, from scratch, themselves, they then own it. What they create may include:

- Printed media - written texts, pictures, drawings, books, articles, magazines or photographs
- Digital media - video games, television, programs or films

This act makes the work of individuals safe from being copied without their permission. Copyright applies to created work, finished work and assets and does not apply to ideas/thoughts or notions.

Copyright is applied automatically when a person creates a piece of work if specific criteria has been met. In the law, it is not necessary for an individual to register a piece of work for copyright, nor is it the law to include there © symbol designating that the work isn't subject to copying. All work, no matter who makes it, is subject to copyright unless they state otherwise. It is there for an 'opt out' law and not an 'opt in'.

Copyright on a piece of work lasts a long time. All copyrights on artistic work, literature, music and film lasts for 70 years after the author/creator's death! When you buy a book, or read an article, the creator is granting you a license to access their work, you are allowed to read it/watch it only. You are not allowed to copy, change or distribute it.

When using a computer, it is illegal to do the following without the creator's permission:

1. Make copies either digitally or printed
2. Sell it on for a profit
3. Sell copies of the material
4. Make a copy and share it with others

Copyright laws apply to music, films, games and television. Since the dawn of broadband in 2001 and the wide use of the internet distributing copies of digital media has been easier. The internet has opened a doorway to illegal sharing through torrents, P2P, and file sharing sites. Even on a computer, if you don't have permission to distribute the asset, you are breaking the law.

There are three instances where a user can in fact copy and distribute material. They are:

- When the asset belongs to you, you made it
- You have the creators expressed consent - the copyright holder has given you permission
- If the copyright holder has given up the copyright and have made the item free to use. This is often called royalty free.

Freedom of Information Act 2000

This act was written to allow members of the public, just like you, to have access to the information held by public authorities. A public authority is an authority with links to the government who provide a public service e.g., councils, schools, refuse collection.

The Freedom of Information Act states that all public authorities must publish certain information about their activities in a place accessible to the public. It also states that any member of the public, should they wish, can request information from the public authority.

The freedom of information act outlines that any member of the public can request access to all or part of an authority's recorded information. Recorded information includes printed documents, computer files, emails, letters, photographs and other digital media such as video and sound.

Public authorities include:

- NHS
- State Schools
- Police
- Local Authorities (councils)
- Government Departments e.g., Department for Work and Pensions

Health and Safety at Work Act 2000

Often regarded as an over cautious act, the Health and Safety at Work Act 1974 is a piece of legislation that covers all aspect of staying safe when in work. The act clearly states the responsibilities of the employer and employee in making sure their working environment is safe. In this act, the employer and the employee must do all that they can to avoid issues arising.

A lot of the act might be common sense, or perceived to be, but it is important that the act is followed to ensure the safety of all.

Below are the responsibilities of the employer and employee within the act:

Employee responsibilities	Employer responsibilities
To take reasonable care of your own and others safety	Ensure health and safety training is undertaken by all staff
Not to interfere or misuse anything that has been provided for your health and safety such as safety equipment	Provide appropriate protective clothing and equipment
To cooperate with your employer by undergoing training, wearing protective clothing and by following health and safety policies	Make sure all facilities meet minimal health and safety requirement in regard to ventilation, temperature and noise
To report any illness or injury that will affect your ability to work	Have an up-to-date health and safety policy
	Maintain a safe working environment by ensuring equipment is properly maintained and safe to use, that appropriate warning signs are displayed and that adequate first aid facilities are available

The Health and Safety at work act helps everyone stay safe at work. When used with the Equality Act, it can ensure that people like me, in a wheelchair are able to safely access a work environment without prejudice or difficulty.

Legislation Summary

For your exam you need to know the following:

- The purpose of each legislation
- Requirements:
    - On individuals, citizens, you, and I to comply with the legislation
    - Businesses, companies, and organisations to comply with the legislation
- What impact does the legislation have on the following:
    - Data and information
    - Individuals, citizens, you, and I
    - Businesses, companies, and organisations
- An understanding of how the legislation can be used when dealing with cyber security issues.

Task:

The UK Government produce a wealth of leaflets, handouts and resources to the public, business, and organisations.

Create a presentation, leaflet, or handout for the Government for each legislation. You may do this with a person in your class. The leaflet must cover:

- The purpose of each legislation
- Requirements of the legislation, its core aims and principles
- The impact the legislation can have on the daily lives of individuals and businesses
- If possible, explain how the legislation can help people and organisations deal with cyber security issues.

Chapter 7: Digital Communications

The world now communicates digitally. We communicate via text, call, instant messaging (IM), social media, video sharing platforms and many other ways. The use of digital communications in the last 30 years has grown rapidly and changed immensely too! In this chapter you will be looking at the various types of digital communications, the ways we use this technology, its target audiences and when a certain communication method may be best and why! Don't assume you know anything, practice, read and learn in this chapter!

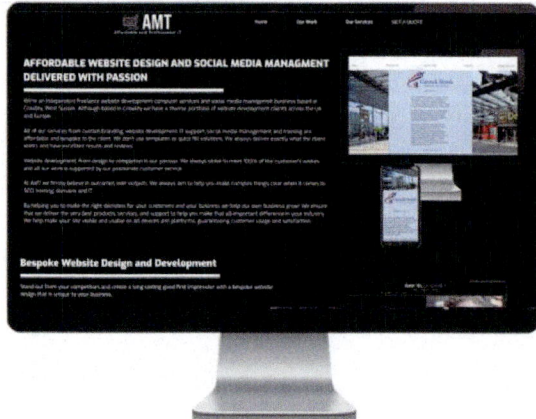

Types of Digital Communications

There are several types of digital communications. They all have one commonality, that is that they all use a computer or device to action, create or distribute the communication medium. You need to know the purpose of each digital communication, the advantages, and disadvantages and finally where this method by be used (in what context).

Image: Websites and Apps are widely used to communicate with clients and customers

Audio

Audio communication is the most common communication type that tends to be overlooked. Audio communication describes any communication done primarily through audio, therefore not having an accompanying image or video. Examples of audio digital communications include, but are not exclusive too:

- Call - calling a person via normal cellular or wired networks
- Podcast - available online and is a audio recording of a conversation or a person's viewpoints
- Radio – Ever since the invention of radio it has been used to digitally communicate current event and the news

Audio is fantastic at explaining a topic, or point of view, it can be accessed in a variety of ways, with little or no subscription. In the UK we have AM, FM and DAB radio, all of these radio frequencies are free of charge meaning it is accessible to everyone with a device to listen in, or is it? Audio is disadvantageous to members of the community with hearing impairments or language barriers. Audio can be used in a wide range of context where visual elements are not required.

Image: Podcast set up, using a microphone as an input device for audio communications

Collaboration Tools

Collaboration tools are tools that are built into computer software that allow multiple to edit the same document or software output at one time. Collaboration tools are now built into all Microsoft Office 365 © packages as well as GSuite © packages from Google. When activated they allow the user to share a document and edit this document with a colleague. This leads to greater team collaboration, greater efficiency, and a higher work output.

However, the user or the user's organisation, need to have signed into these systems and in some instances purchased licences to enable the collaboration to work. Poor internet connection, or a lack of internet connection will also make the tools inaccessible and so the user or their organisation also require a stable internet connection. The requirement for licences and an internet connection makes this digital communication type paid for and not free.

Infographics

Infographics enhance the reading of the user. They demonstrate, visually, the writers' thoughts and information. An infographic can enable non-native speakers and those with language barriers to access information. This is because ethe infographic often is a simplistic, diagrammatical representation. They can be used in presentations and on websites and apps. Sometimes they are used as links or buttons indicating that the clicking of the graphic will lead to information on the that topic.

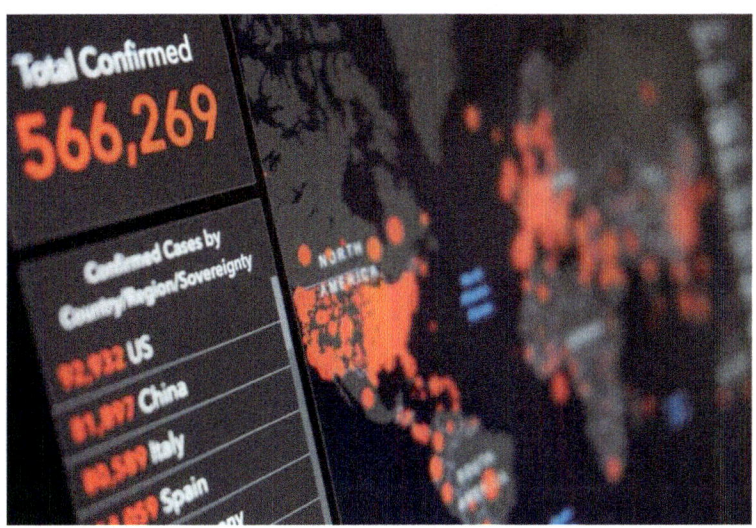

However, they can be confusing and misleading. Sometimes, an infographic that makes perfect sense to author will not make sense to a novice user. This can cause further confusion than if the infographic hadn't been used at all.

Infographics were widely used in the covid-19 global pandemic. Using colours, dots and visual representations allows the public to understand otherwise complex and difficult data.

Task:

In 1854, Dr John Snow created a map. This map, long before digital communication used infographics to help the user understand the data.

Research this map, explain what the map showed and what the use of infographics meant to this important maps huge success.

Social Media

Social media today plays a large part in our lives. Facebook, Instagram, Twitter, TikTok, Snap Chat are all household names. These social media platforms have only been in our present lives for around 15-20 years! Yet their invention, and introduction into our world have changed digital communications forever.

Advantages of social media:

- Allow quick communication between people who may not be geographically close
- Allow for new connections to be made
- Provide people with an ability to witness a loved ones or friends life
- Allow businesses to reach a wide audience quickly and in a targeted way
- Allow businesses to be accessible to their customer base with instant responses and messages

Disadvantages of social media:

- Causes a greater divide between people and business who are on the platform and are not
- Can lead to a 'pseudo reality' where people only see what is posted online and not the reality
- Can be used for the distribution of hateful material and mistruths (fake news)
- Can be used to victimise or bully someone
- Users must have an account and internet connection to access the platform

Social media has changed the way we communicate and access material. With all social media now being used for business advertisement it has made the consumer and company closer than ever before. It can be used for great work such as charity work, outreach work and jobs. Like everything else, it can also be used for negative aspects too, hate crimes and the distribution of hateful information against a person, or a group, or a race of people.

Did you know?

In a 2018 survey by Facebook. 94% of users stated that the first thing they did when they woke up in a morning was check either, Facebook, Instagram, or Whats App! What do you think the first thing someone did in 1998 was before social media existed?

Video

Video sharing platforms such as YouTube © and TikTok © have hanged digital communications. In 2018 users of YouTube © out 'watched' content on the platform to tradition TV. The rise of YouTube © has left many people questioning the future of film and TV with our attention spans changing and the expectation for instant information access now being normal.

Advantages of video:

- Opens the playing field of influences on everyday life. This allows professionals in all sectors to share their knowledge with the world at the click of a button
- Helpful when sued to learn or gain new information
- Useful for businesses to share information with their customers through adverts or reviews
- Useful for business such as Ikea © to support customers in an interactive way
- Often platforms allow the inclusion of closed captions (cc) for the hearing impaired and has audio for the visually impaired

Disadvantages of social media:

- It is not rated. By this it means any material is accessible to anyone of any age. Unlike TV, Film and Games, online video communication platforms allow users to post what they want anyone to see.
- It is not regulated or censored. This allows anybody to share a video with their feelings, thoughts and 'truths' for the world to see. This can lead to a rise in the spreading of mistruths or the rise in far-right groups such as America First and Britain First who are able to share material freely with people without warning or restriction.

Task:

Taking TikTok and the rise of TikTok in 2020 as a case study can you discuss the impact of video sharing platforms on digital communications?

Discuss the:

- Positive impacts on people and business
- Negative impacts on people and business

Voice over Internet Protocol (VoIP)

Voice over Internet Protocol, also more commonly known as VoIP, refers to making phone calls solely over the internet rather than through a mobile phone signal or landline.

In the digital communication revolution VoIP has taken over from normal telephony and there are clear reasons why. Firstly, it is much cheaper than regular phone lines. The service is provided by your internet connection, it doesn't charge you extra for use and there is no cap on the number of minutes you spend on the phone.

There are three common VoIP systems they are:

1. A regular phone with a VoIP adaptor. The special VoIP adapter act as a converter and allow digital data to pass through to the device via its usual phone line connection.
2. A device that has access to the internet e.g. a tablet, PC, or laptop. Examples include Google Talk, Apple Facetime and Skype along with newcomers WhatsApp calls and Facebook Messenger calling. Essentially this technology allows the user to call another without using the air waves or landline, they use the user's internet connection.
3. Smart Phones - All smart phones have a 3G, 4G or 5G connection. This means, when using one of the many apps on the market, smart phones can make use of VoIP for digital communication

Key Vocabulary:
- Smart Phone
- VoIP
- Social Media
- Infographic
- Collaboration tools
- Digital Communication

Distribution Channels

The ways in which information and communication is distributed largely depends on the distribution channel. There are several channels to be aware of. For the exam you need to know the advantages and disadvantages of each as well as the context in which they might be used. The distribution channels are below:

- Cloud
- Email
- Messaging
- Mobile Apps
- Multimedia
- VoIP
- Websites

We have already discussed mobile app and websites in chapter 2, but the other distribution methods are slightly different as explained below:

Cloud

Cloud storage (see chapter 2) is a digital communication distribution channel because it allows people in different geographical location access to the same material. This is advantageous to business as their employees can work anywhere at any time. However, an internet connection is still required, and a device suitable to work is also required which can put strain on the users if they are required to use the channel with no extra support. In addition, there is an argument that cloud storage has led to a shift in 'work/life balance' seeing people working more from home than ever before. It is great for individuals to share files and for businesses to have centralised storage that is accessible anywhere on the planet with an internet connection.

Email

Email is a perfect example of modern communication. With a global population of 7.2 billion people there are 3.9 billion daily email users. This number is expected to climb to 4.3 billion by 2023. This shows the usage of email as a communication channel. Emails are simple, quick and convenient. They can be sued to communicate with anyone at anytime and happen in 'real time'. In many modern companies there are complaints of 'death by email; where a shift has happened and there is now and over reliance on email rather than speaking. Email also have built in filtering which may be inadvertently stop certain emails from getting into a person's inbox. This can be both advantages and disadvantageous.

Multimedia

Multimedia is a wide umbrella term used to describe images, video, gif, and sound. Multimedia can be used in a variety of ways and often used to support text to enhance the readers understanding of a topic or context. Some multimedia can lead to confusion unless the user has some prior knowledge. For example, the use of certain emoji's may be confusing unless the emoji's alternative meaning is known.

Connection Methods

Simple stating that digital communication methods use the internet isn't specific enough. Within the bracket of internet connections, we have several different ways in which we can access the internet. They are:

4G / 5G

We all use this connectivity method; this is the way in which we connect to the internet via our smart phones or tablets. In the last 15 years we have seen the roll out of 3G, 4G and recently 5G. With each iteration or 'generation' (that's what the G stands for) the internet speed has increased. This has been due to the demand of the users, more streaming, gaming and working means a higher requirement for the internet speed.

Connections are made between the device and a cellular signal tower or generator. The signal generator outputs the signal and the nearer the user the better the signal. This form of communication does have its weaknesses. Often users in remote areas, or in rural areas struggle for signal.

Task:

Use Google to look for 'dead' spots in your mobile network's coverage.

Google 'nperf, UK signal map' and do some wider research. What are the dead spots? Are there any common links?

Bluetooth

Bluetooth is a short-range wireless technology that was released in 1994! Being one of the older connection methods for digital communication, Bluetooth has been on a transformative journey since its roll-on Sony Eriksen devices in the mid 90's. Initially used for wireless communication devices that allowed users to connect an earpiece to their cellular device Bluetooth changed the world. It allowed users to ring and answer calls at the touch of a button. It also allowed users to continue always using two hands because it removed the need for them to use one hand to hold their phone.

In the early to mid 00's Bluetooth was most widely used for short distance file transfer. Two devices, in direct line of sight, could share songs, images and documents easily and for free. During this time businesses also used Bluetooth for the sharing of promotional material, they targeted shoppers who had Bluetooth on as they passed by their shops.

In today's climate, Bluetooth is most widely used for wireless headphone and in car connectivity. Taking into consideration all of the different types of digital communications listed earlier in this chapter, Bluetooth allows any audio to be shared more easily, that's video and audio e.g. podcast, calls, VoIP.

Mobile Wi-Fi hotspots

A mobile WiFi hotspot are a separate device that can be carried easily in a user's pocket or bag. They are small and light and have their own battery that is chargeable. The hotspots use a SIM card, like a smart phone, to connect to 3G, 4G and 5G signals. They transmit these signals to devices that want to connect to it like a traditional router.

They are good for devices that don't have cellular connections like laptops, computers, or tablets. They allow the user to access the internet when away from a WiFi network.

Negatively, these devices often can't be used for extensive web browsing. They are best used for quick work or document access via collaboration tools. SIM data plans can be expensive per Gb of data downloaded. These devices often come with a download limit to, which if exceeded can cost the user a lot of money.

Wi-Fi

WiFi is used to wirelessly connect to the internet. It is useable over short distances and often only used in a Local Area Network (LAN), sometimes Metropolitan Area Networks (MAN) will use WiFi and this can be seen in town centres where there is a council WiFi to use.

WiFi transmits the information through radio waves, the router sends the signal, and the devices Network Interface Card (NIC) receives it.

There are two variations of WiFi. 2G and 5G. Most home routers now have these, and you can see them in the WiFi menu on your phone. The 2G variant is stronger over longer distances, it can pass through obstacles more easily and so should be used the further away from the router that you are. The 5G variety is faster but is best when you are in the same room as the router and multiple devices are in one area connected to the router.

Task:

WiFi can have many barriers between the router and the end user's device. Walls, doors, microwaves, and soft furnishings all affect the signal.

Thinking about Science and the science of signals, absorption, and refraction, explain why WiFi struggles over great distances or in different buildings made of different materials.

Wired

Wired networks are the most common networks in Computer Science and IT. Wired connections use several different wire types to form their connections. They are:

- Copper
    - Coaxial
    - Twisted Pair
- Fibre

The wire used is dependent on the characteristics of the network. The network manager will ask the following questions before they select a wire:

1. What data is going to be transmitted?
2. How far will the data be transmitted?
3. How many users are there?
4. Where will the wire be house/laid/installed?

Copper

Coaxial (coax) Cables

Coaxial cables, commonly known as coax, are cables that have been used for digital communication transmission for over 70 years. However coaxial cables were first invented in 1880 and they were sued to transmit telephone conversations!

The structure of the cable is important. The coax cable has an inner copper cable knows as a conductor. The conductor is surrounded by another conducting shield. The name coaxial becomes because these two elements share a common geometric axis.

These cables are used for:

- TV – Freeview Aerials, Sky Set Top Boxes, and Virgin Media
- Internet – Many fibres optic providers don't provide the fibre to the user's house. They run fibre to a transmission box and then coaxial cable to the users house.
- Data transmission – Data transmission between buildings and businesses that are geographically close.

Coaxial cable can go around 45-100m without any signal loss. As they can take high bandwidths of signal and large amounts of data, they are perfect of larger LAN's.

Twisted Pair

Invented by Alexander Graham Bell, twisted pair cables are called this because they have two conductors, copper cables, that are twisted together.

Unshielded Twisted Pair (UTP)

> Who was Alexander Graham Bell?

The word unshielded in their name should suggest what these are. They are two copper cables with no plastic shielding that are twisted together. The cables are twisted together in pairs so that new connections can be added as and when required. This was revolutionary when invented because it allowed a network to grow and grow! Your home telephone, the landline, used UTP and so if your internet comes through your phone line, it too uses UTP for its connection. The UTP cable will have several cables within it twisted together. Each pair is given a different coloured sleeve or jacket. The colour corresponds to the cable's quality allowing network engineers to effectively use the cables as required.

Advantages of UTP:

1. Cost effective for business
2. Easy to install and install discreetly
3. Use for short distances up to 100m for more modern UTP and 25m for older UTP cables

Disadvantages of UTP:

1. They do not provide a secure connection
2. Boosters are required every 100m
3. The cables have a limited bandwidth

Shielded Twisted Pair (STP)

Unlike their unshielded counterparts these cables have an extra layer of insulation, an extra shield from the outside world. This shield comes in the form of a copper braid covering, it provides structural strength to the cable an d reused noise and signal interference. The STP too has colour coded pairs however they designate analogue and digital signals instead of cable quality. These STP cables are very costly and hard to install.

Advantages of UTP:

1. Great for longer distance communications – usually installed underground
2. The protective shield prevents external electromagnetic noise penetration into the cable.
3. They have a higher bandwidth

Disadvantages of UTP:

1. They are very expensive (per metre)
2. They require continued maintenance
3. They can only be installed underground

So where can UTP and STP cables be used, in what context?

1. Telephony – telephone lines
2. Local Area Networks (LA) use UTP cables known as Cat5+ cabling
3. They can be us e for both analogue and digital signals

Fibre

Fibre cabling, also commonly known as fibre optic, is a form of cabling that uses light to transmit data. The light signal travels through the cable which is made of a glass tube core shielded with plastic for protection.

Like its copper cable counterparts, fibre cable sends pulses of light from one location to another. The pulse either designates a 1 or a 0 which the computer can use to understand the digital data sent.

Fibre optic cables come in different grades with some being able to travel for up to 400/500m without signal regeneration. This along with their ability to use large amounts of bandwidth makes them great for high-speed internet. Fibreoptic cables can send up to 40Gb per second from one location to another making the common 500mbps broadband a walk in the park!

Task:

Fibre optics are sued in networking for their speed and distance. However, companies such as Virgin Media provide fibre optic broadband. Research the following:

- What is fibre optic internet?
- What are the advantages of fibre optic internet?
- What are the disadvantages of fibre optic internet?
- What does the term 'fibre to the box' mean?
- What does the term 'fibre to the door' mean?

Chapter 8: The Internet of Everything (IoE)

The Internet of Everything is a term used widely within the Computer Science and IT industry. It refers to the use of internet enabled devices to better the connections between people, business and society.

This umbrella term refers to all of the devices that we use in our everyday lives that connect to the internet. Our phones, tables, TV's, games consoles, home assistants. All these devices expand our connections and digital presence. The IoE is a philosophy, a theory, and isn't something that you can see or touch.

It explores the prospect that the future of our world is built up of many different appliances, devices, items, and business sectors all connected to one global internet connection and the power that this prospect can bring.

Task:

Create a list of all the internet enabled and connected devices in your home. Consider:

- Devices
- Appliances
- Gadgets

The Four Pillars of the IoE

The philosophy uses the analogy of a building to create a visual representation. This building is supported by four pillars, each integral to the buildings structure.

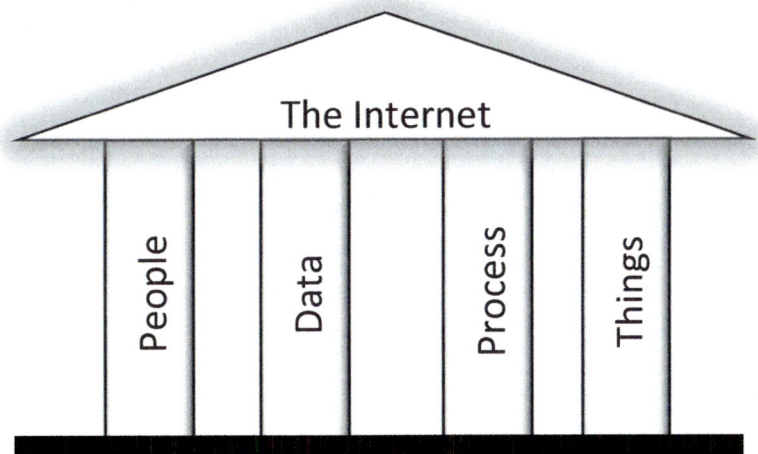

In a building the pillars are instrumental to the longevity of the structure. Likewise, in the representation shown above the pillars are important to the success of the internet itself. Each pillar alone can not support the internet, it is their interconnection between themselves that can support the internet and make it worthwhile.

People

That's us, society, you and I. If the internet doesn't have people suing it, contributing to it and experiencing it, it will fail. Think of a website, let's say our eLearning website www.amt-elearning.co.uk, if people don't visit it what will happen? It will not be seen or used and search engines won't think it's a reliable source of information. In not thinking it's a reliable source of information it will not be used and so the vicious circle begins. The people visit are important, but the people updating are too, like the people visiting if people don't update the site with new content, then the site will become outdated and old.

Data

The people not updating the information, or data on a website will lead to old, outdated data. This will lead to people not wanting to sue the website because its data isn't reliable or trustworthy and so as you can see these pillars are directly interconnected. Data refers to any facts, figures and information recalled by a device when requested. This data must be relevant and trustworthy.

> Have you ever had the experience where you have found something on a search engine like a price, opening times or telephone number only to later find out it was wrong? How did you feel? Did you trust that website in the future?

Process

A process is a set of rules, rules that must be adhered to for something to succeed. A process you will have experienced is tying your shoes. You know that there must be an action that precedes the creation of two loops. You can tie your shoes with just the two loops, but it isn't as strong and is prone to failure. The processes used in a computer are similar, and the ones that are needed for the internet to function are too. These processes may be referred to as protocols. Sometimes, these protocols fail, have you ever seen an Error 404 page on a website? Too many failed processes can be an indication of poor data and can lead to a reduction in the number of people accessing your site.

Things

Probably the vaguest name within the four pillars, things refer to the devices used to connect to the internet. It also includes network devices and infrastructure. Whilst having the vaguest name, it is the least vague pillar to understand. Essentially, without a device to access the internet, a user (the people) can access the processes which connects them with the data. Imagine using a old laptop to play a game on, or an old mobile to add an app. If the device doesn't allow the user to access the information, it isn't worthwhile using.

Internet of Things and The Internet of Everything

The Internet of Things (IoT) is vastly different to the Internet of Everything (IoE). The IoT refers to the interconnection between things/devices and focusses on this one pillar. Whereas the IoE focusses on further aspects known as pillars.

Task:

Create a timeline using images and explanations of the development of things since 2000.

IoE digital interactivity

There are two different interactions that take place within the IoE. Interactions are what happens when 2 or more components use one another or communicate between one another. These interactions are categorised as device to device and device to human.

Device to Device

Can you think of a time where two devices interact? You may not even realise, but devices interact all the time. My doorbell interacts with my phone via an app, my phone can 'cast' an image to my TV, my home assistant can turn on lights, change a thermostat, ring a taxi, order a takeaway, well, it can do a lot actually! All the device-to-device interactions are due to the processes in place for the internet. The internet acts as a gateway, a portal, allowing different devices to communicate.

Device to Human

Device to human interaction is covered extensively in chapter 1. Regarding the IoE, our devices, our things, provide a mode of transport for digital data to become understood and seen. The HCI largely plays a part in the way in which humans understand the data presented to them, however without the device understanding the digital data the HCI can't start to present it. You have device to human interaction every time you open an internet enabled app, browse the internet, social media, or video sharing platform.

Task:

1. Using chapter 2 to support you, can you explain how the IoE can be sued differently, but advantageously, for users with additional needs
2. Using chapter 1 to support you explain how the IoE and its use of HCI might differ from device to device and user to user.

Applications of the IoE

As you will have already established the IoE is widely used both in terms of people and industry as well as geographically. The users can be categorised into the following groups:

Industry	Possible Uses	Advantages	Disadvantages
Energy Management	• Thermostatic control • Wireless water shut off • Solar energy • Hydro energy	• Allows for remote control of different energy management systems • Can be used to control central heating systems more effectively and environmentally friendly	• Relies on an internet connection • Can be subject of a cyber attack
Health	• WiFi Stethoscope • Remote appointments • WiFi pacemaker • Online Training	• Makes healthcare more accessible • Support for people remotely • Allows more people to receive medical help at a given time	• Relies on an internet connection • Can be subject of a cyber attack • Some health complaints can't be diagnosed dover the phone/camera
Manufacturing	• Warehouse Glasses • WiFi Hardhat • Automation • Robotics	• Can improve output and productivity • Allows for better working conditions	• Can lead to staff redundancies • Reliant on the internet connection • No liability should the wrong process be followed
Business	• Websites • Apps • Booking services • eCommerce	• Can lead to a wider customer demographic • Higher revenue streams • Easier to track inventory	• Removes face to face sales • Needs financial investment • Reliant on the internet connection • No liability should the wrong process be followed
Home	• Home assistant • Automation • Security	• Lower energy bills • Interconnected lifestyle • Higher standard of living • Easier access to information	• Needs financial investment • Reliant on the internet connection • Can be unresponsive
Personal	• Smart watch • Smart phone • Tablet • Wearables	• Ease of access to information • Interconnected lifestyle • Higher standard of living • Higher safety levels	• Needs financial investment • Reliant on the internet connection • Can be inaccurate • Device may be stolen
Transport	• Ticket acquisition • Electric vehicles • Driverless vehicles	• Ease of access to services • Higher standard of living • Higher safety levels	• Reliant on the internet connection • No liability should the wrong process be followed • Danger to public if it fails

Task:

Just like we have done above, create your own table for the category of Military and Emergency Services. Emergency services include:

Ambulance, Coastguard, Fire Service, Mountain Rescue, Police

R070: Using Augmented Reality to present Information

What is Augmented Reality?

Augmented Reality is the placing of a digital layer over existing reality, between the user's eye and the real world. It is different to Virtual Reality which uses a headset to transport a user into another world, a digital world. Augmented Reality has made it possible for us to share information with users in infinite more detail than before. It allows us to show 2D and 3D items in the world we already live in. These items can have multiple layers and information to explore and discover.

AR makes interaction with products easier and in turn makes audiences more engaged with the product or topic. A range of businesses from IT, architecture, retail, hospitality, education, and government can use AR to communicate with their key audiences.

AR experiences are built on software development kits called SDK's. The coursework 'R070: Using Augmented Reality to present information' will allow you to learn the basics of AR and you will create a prototype of an AR app in an SDK.

Task:

So, what is reality? How do we define realty? If reality is something you can see and hear, then realty is nothing more than two senses sending electrical signals to your brain. If we add the other senses of taste, touch, and smell into the mix, surely a 4D cinema is therefore real and the experience you are having is real. But what is your definition of real?

Questions:

What is Augmented Reality to you? If we think about apps such as Pokémon Go, Harry potter Wizards Unite or the 'filters' that you can apply in Snap Chat, what is reality for you?

Thinking about the following areas of business, how do you think they could use Augmented Reality?

Architecture –

Education –

Entertainment –

Retail –

Lifestyle -

AR In Architecture

By combining data-rich 3D models and real-world building sites, AR in architecture lets teams connect and collaborate at every phase of design and construction. It allows architects to plan more effectively by seeing what an area may look like with the planned structure in place before it is even built!

Using AR models allow the designers and builders to explore new structures, trial/simulate new mechanical structures, challenge existing knowledge on variables and input different 'fields' of data to see how they may appear.

It has been suggested that AR has untold potential in allowing architects and engineer to model and experiment with their designs that allow them to troubleshoot any issues digitally rather than.

Uses of AR in Architecture

Project Planning

For architects and designers, AR offers much of its value in the early stages of design as a tool to experiment with form and attract client and stakeholder buy-in. It helps non-designers understand how any architectural composition will work: the proportion of spaces, its orientation on a site, the views it affords, the mix of material finishes. AR is excellent for this use, as it allows anyone to "walk the site" long before breaking ground. *Research the software ARKi and explain what it does*

Real-Time Collaboration

The COVID-19 pandemic has made everyone an expert in remote, real-time collaboration; AR is yet another technology pushing this frontier. *Research the software Virtualist and explain what it does for the user*

Underground Construction

Given its ability to peel back layers and discern what's hidden, AR technology is ideal for underground construction projects. Instead of sorting through reams of blueprints hidden away in a government office basement, AR allows builders to create dynamic and accurate models of what's underground, seeing how perilous it might be to bring an excavator around.

> **Explain** how the construction of Crossrail in London may have used AR in the early stages.

Facility Operations and Maintenance

The need to keep a close eye on a building doesn't stop after its grand opening; AR inspection by operations and maintenance staff can help prolong a building's life. Having an updatable digital model to follow through the years can give staff a superb picture of how the building operated when it was brand new and how it's changed over the years.

AR in Education

AR in education is revolutionizing the classroom and learning experience internationally. AR allows for immersive engagement with otherwise difficult topic areas. Science experiments, practical electronics, and trips to places of interest or historic importance are all possible from within the classroom with little extra kit or training required.

Augmented Reality (AR) in education features aspects that enhance learning of abilities like problem-solving, collaboration, and creation to better prepare students for the future. It is also good for traditional pedagogy focused on technical knowledge and proficiencies.

Key benefits of AR in Education:

1. Reading – AR makes reading immersive and engaging. Changing the delivery method of the content and user interaction.
2. Spatial Concepts – Increasing students' awareness of the relationship between humans and objects. AR brings reality to the unseen, the delivery of topics such as space can be delivered engagingly and with enhanced user experiences/interactions.
3. Working with numbers – visualising the working number processes can be difficult. AR brings working with numbers alive and in front of the students' eyes
4. Learn through play – Often forgotten, but navigating and playing with an object, physical or digital engages parts of the human mind that doesn't become engaged through reading alone.

Task: If only…

Since picking your GCSE options you have seen the number of subjects you study drop and you are now, supposedly, studying only subjects you want to.

Make a list of areas that you think could use AR and would benefit from using AR in your teaching. When you have made your list explain each point taking into consideration why it would be beneficial and how it would be beneficial.

Here is an example:

Internal components of a computer - This would be beneficial because it would allow me to build a computer, check if it works and see the internal components easily. The normal way to do this would be with real components, this is a health and safety risk due to electric shock. AR would allow me to visually see the components and build the computer.

Augmented Reality in the Entertainment Industry

The entertainment industry is huge. Humans have sought entertainment in many different ways for centuries from the Romans and their bloody amphitheatres to Shakespeare and his plays and now the modern Netflix and chill we like to be entertained. For this section of Augmented Reality uses we will break it down into the following sections.

1. Gaming
2. Movies/Film and TV
3. Applications

Gaming

This must be the first section of AR uses those springs to mind right? With the release of Pokémon Go in 2016 and then subsequent games over the last 5 years Augmented Reality has taken our gaming to new levels. However, many times, AR and VR are confused, and this is a problem. Remember:

- AR provides a layer over reality
- VR uses technology to place the user in an alternate reality
- In recent years AR has also been used in board game design and is now hugely popular with Escape Rooms

Task: Explain the R's

XR = AR + VR + MR

Task: Here are some applications of AR in gaming. Take each and explain how they use AR and the purpose of AR in the game itself. Try to explain the 'role' AR plays in the game, is it a perk, an add on or is it fundamental.

- Pokémon Go
- Harry Potter Wizards Unite
- Jurassic World Alive
- Angry Birds Isle of Pigs
- Tilt Five

AR in Movies/TV and Film

Augmented Reality has featured in films for over 30 years! Which is really interesting to think about when we are only just beginning to see this in our every day lives.

One of the earliest films to show AR was Top Gun in 1986 with Tom Cruise. It is expected that this was a feature because AU has been used in fighter jets since the 1970s. They show a scope/target marker which is an overlay on reality to show the pilot where the bullet they are about to fire will hit, perfect for firing at the opposition.

Below are a list of films that have famously shown AR in them. Explore these films and suggest why they used AR:

- They live
- Total Recall
- Terminator
- Minority Report
- Avatar

Famously, Iron man uses AR to communicate with Jarvis, his personal computer assistant. Can you explain why AR, when used in films, gives the suggestion to the audience of futuristic technology? Can you extend your explanation to discuss how AR engages the audience and allows them to see, hear and feel more from a 2D film?

Finally, what TV shows have used AR in them, use a search engine to find five TV shows that have used AR and explain what AR was used form. To start you off here is o ne for free, The 100.

AR in Retail

The retail world has changed dramatically since the widespread use of the internet for eCommerce and sales.

The high street stores we once used regularly are dropping from the shopping centres every year. BHS, Woolworths, HMV, Debenhams, H & M and New Look all are either closing completely or dramatically reducing their store numbers. But why?

Going shopping used to be an event, something to do, shoppers perused the shelves, tried on the items and bought things for their homes that they happened upon during their trip to the shops.

Augmented Reality has changed the shopping experience again with users now being able to try on products virtually, selecting a garment from an online store and placing them on a static image of themselves or on themselves in live time.

Ikea started allowing users to see 3D products in their homes in 2018. Since then, DIY website builder Shopify too has allowed users to insert an item into their homes to see if they like it before they buy it, gone are the days of returning items that don't fit or work!

AR allows shoppers to have live information in store. It is estimated that nearly 60% of shoppers check out a product on their phone, in store, before they purchase. American Apparel launched their AR app, and it has been downloaded over 1 million times internationally, showing that this can have a huge reach when customers do visit the store as well as online.

Before its closure, Top Shop install virtual fitting rooms in their stores. This full-length mirror allowed shoppers to stand in front of it and interactively select an item of clothing to super impose on themselves, without the need for undressing!

AR in lifestyle

Lifestyle is an umbrella term for everyday life! So, we have discussed the use of AR in most sectors of our everyday lives looking at specific categories.

How else may we use AR in our everyday lives?

Below are AMT's top everyday uses of AR, globally, not necessarily yours or ours everyday uses we must say!

Augmented Reality in the Military

Integrated Visual Augmentation System (IVAS) is being developed by Microsoft in partnership with the US Army to improve soldiers' situational awareness, comms, battlefield navigation, and overall operational efficiency.

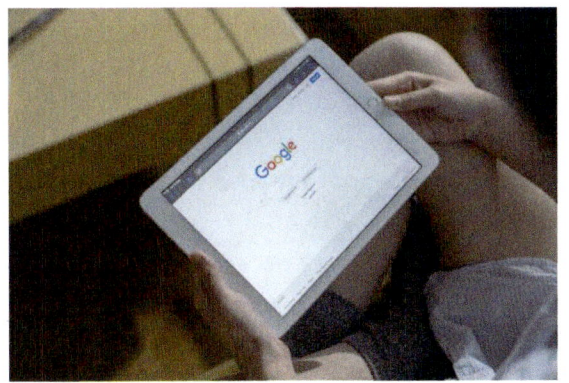

AR in Search

3D Animals are another interesting application of AR technology. Google 3D animals allows you to find and view life-sized animals in 3D as well as interact with them in your local space using augmented reality.

AR in Fashion

Asos' See My Fit technology uses augmented reality to virtually fit clothing onto models. It enables you to see exactly how products fit by trying up to 500 products per week on six models. This way you can visualise the size, fit, and cut of each apparel before you pay.

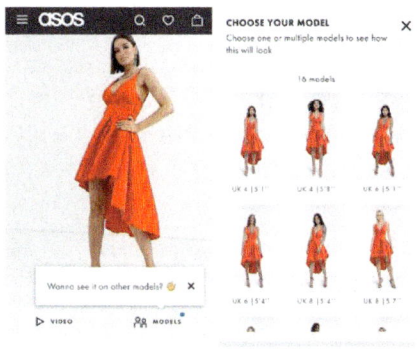

3D Colouring Books

Disney's augmented reality colouring book app allows you to draw your favourite characters in 2D on paper, and have them rendered in 3D in real-time. Using texture generation, the app matches and duplicates sections of the drawing in 3D. With deformable surface tracking, you can move your characters as you turn the pages.

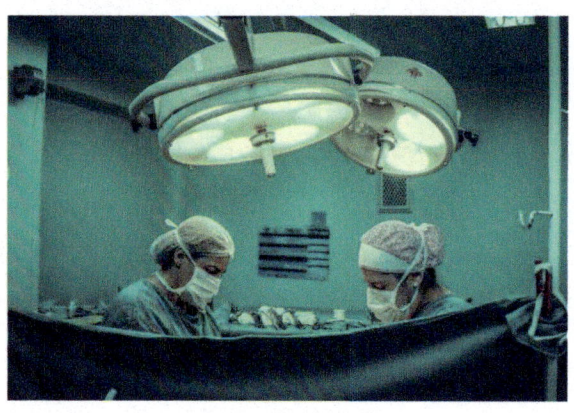

Medicine

Road to Birth is an AR+VR project being developed by the Innovation Team at the University of Newcastle, Australia, to provide visual insights into the stages of childbearing and its effects on pregnant women.

Sports

Imagine team set plays displayed right in front of you in 3D, pre-game practice with computer-generated opponents, virtual training environments, custom-built training sets for individual athletes, and much more.

Car Sales

AR can help you to drive showroom visits and car sales, better communicate technical details about a car or its components to your sales team and customers, and more. Engine Creative implemented "X-Ray car AR" technology for Delphi at the Automechanika show in Frankfurt. Visitors to the exhibition stand were able to scan, visualize, and interact with a life-sized 3D image of a Honda Civic, to better understand how Delphi products work under the hood— boosting customer engagement and sales.

AR in applications

Since its launch in 2011 Snap Chat has changed the way, we take images and selfies. The use of AR in applications like Snap Chat, WhatsApp, Facebook Messenger and Instagram have allowed us to edit and modify the way we appear on the camera with the click of a button. This form of AR, where we place a digital layer over the real image has led to changes in the law whereby images are no longer as reliable as they used to be.

Initially, Snap Chat said that the release of filters such as dog ears and cats' noses was for pure entertainment and humour, more recently a survey of user s aged 13-19 said they used Snap Chat filters because it made them 'more attractive'

> **Ask yourself...**
>
> So what's the attraction? Why is this entertaining? why do we use them?
>
> What is the impact of this on society?

Negative Impacts of AR

There have been several instances where AR and its use has been negative to people and to society. In these tasks, you need to reflect on the negative aspects of AR.

Since its release, it has been reported that there have been over 20 deaths associated with Pokémon Go. many of these deaths were as a result of people not observing their surroundings or attempting to reach an in-game character dangerously.

Discuss the negative impacts of AR games such as Pokémon Go and explain how AR can cause distraction from normal reality.

It has been widely reported that use of filters in applications such as Snap Chat and Instagram has resulted in lower self-opinions and an impact on teenage self-image (what society deems as attractive).

> **Task:**
>
> Explain, from your perspective, the ways AR filters could lead to these opinions and a change in the human perception of beauty/normality

Types of Augmented Reality and user interaction

There are three different versions of AR. To the average user, it is easy to not see any variation in these differences, but these slight differences often make a huge difference to the output of the game and most of all the context that it is used in.

1. The three types of AR are:
2. Object recognition / Marker-based
3. Location based / Marker less
4. Superimposed

Object Recognition/Marker Based

This type of AR, also known as object recognition-based AR or image recognition, relies on identification of markers/user-defined images to function.

Marker-based AR requires a marker to activate an augmentation (something that appears on the devices screen for the suer to see).

Markers are distinct patterns that cameras can easily recognise and process and are visually independent of the environment around them; they can be paper-based or physical objects that exist in the real world.

Maker-based AR works by scanning a marker which triggers an augmented experience (whether an object, text, video or animation) to appear on the device. It usually requires software in the form of an app, which enables users to scan markers from their device using its camera feed.

Location Based/Marker less

- Marker less Augmented Reality is the name used to describe an AR application that doesn't need prior knowledge of a user's environment to overlay 3D content into a scene and hold it to a fixed point in space.
- Augmented Reality has completed the transition from image- or QR code-based activations to marker less Augmented Reality experiences in the last 5 years
- Apple's ARKit and Google's ARCore SDKs have made marker less AR available on hundreds of millions of smartphones and tablets.
- Retailers, educators and game producers are a few of the groups currently leveraging marker less AR to create amazing tools and content.

Marker-based AR apps use markers (target images) to indicate things in a given space. These markers determine where the AR application places digital 3D content within the user's visual field or through a camera feed.

Marker less AR places virtual 3D objects in the physical environment depending on the environment's real features rather than identifying markers.

Marker less AR experiences are possible because of advancements in cameras, sensors, processors, and algorithms capable of accurately detecting and mapping the real-world.

Superimposed

Superimposition based AR provides an 'alternate' view of the object in concern, either by replacing the entire view with an augmented view of the object or by replacing a portion of the object view with an augmented view.

This technology can be used for multiple purposes.

1. Doctors can use the technology to examine the patient from various angles in real-time. A live feed from an X-Ray machine can be used to superimpose the X-Ray view of the patient's body part on the real image to provide better understanding of the damage to bones. The application can be made to work via a head mounted display or special goggles.
2. In military applications, superimposition-based AR can provide multiple views of a target object without showing extra information in text and blocking the vision of soldier from other important objects around. If you have been shooting enemies via your computer mouse, you'd already know how it would appear. Superimposition of infrared view or radioactive view of an object or an area can help save lives; or win wars!
3. Superimposition of ancient pictures over real ones can provide interesting views of historical places. Broken monuments can come back to life in all their original glory.
4. To allow a tiger or snake near you might be a horrifying experience with hazardous consequences, except when superimposition AR is used to bring them to you.

> **Task:** It is hard, in fact it is impossible, to predict the future. However, taking into consideration our current Human Computer Interfaces, how do you think AR might impact this in the next 20 or 30 years?
>
> Create a plan called 'Tomorrow's User Interface' and explain what you think the interfaces of tomorrow might look like.
>
> - Some points to consider are:
> - Menus and user selection
> - Media such as images, videos, and sound
> - User experience
>
> Your plan can be completed digitally, although this will be tough. Try and do this on paper and include different annotated drawings to explain your AR UI of tomorrow. Make sure you use some key terminology from this course.

Layers/User Interaction

Action Flow

You control the device.

Any interaction through AR will involve users to either command verbally, tap on the virtual buttons or navigate through the menu. This involves costs associated with every gesture that yield results. The cost of interaction largely defines the user experience, and one way to gauge it is to have a user flow in place.

Action flow refers to ever changing aspects of the AR because of the user's input. Action allows may be used to describe the popular AR game Pokémon Go, the action used by the user would be tap and select but the camera also acts as a input feeding the superimposition image on the users screen.

Static

You see the data

Static visualisations require less control and project data visualisations to the user.

Often graphical, a graph or chart, these visualisations are shared with users and are swiped through to explain difficult data concepts.

They may also be used to explain the data or for data modelling.

Interactive

Allows the user to explore

This is the AR commonly shown in the movies and on TV. It allows the user to interact with elements that they couldn't without the AR. Think Iron Man and Jarvis. Iron man can simulate outcomes and look at the component structure of a range of items, but the items are never in front of him.

Interactive AR is becoming increasingly popular in engineering, allowing engineers to see what the structure will look like and be like when completed or before they investigate.

Glossary

3D - 3D modeling is the process of developing a mathematical coordinate-based representation of any surface of an object in three dimensions via specialised software by manipulating edges, vertices, and polygons in a simulated 3D

4G - 4G is the fourth generation of wireless mobile telecommunications technology

5G - 5G is the fifth generation of wireless mobile telecommunications technology

---

A

Access rights - Restricting employees access to certain files, folders or network areas depending on their job, role or permissions.

Adware - Adware, often called advertising-supported software by its developers, is software that generates revenue for its developer by automatically generating online advertisements in the user interface

Alpha Testing - Alpha testing is the initial phase of validating whether a new product will perform as expected

Alphanumeric - A data type used when the data is a combination of letters and numbers

Anti-virus - Antivirus is a kind of software used to prevent, scan, detect and delete viruses from a computer

App- shortened from application. An app is a specific piece of software used on a mobile device such as a tablet or phone.

Assistive Technology - technology that is used to assist someone with a disability or access issue.

Audio - Name given to describe any sound emitted from the computer. Describes sounds, warning, and alerts.

Augmented Reality - is an experience where designers enhance parts of users' physical world with computer-generated input.

B

Baiting - A type of social engineering attack where a scammer uses a false promise to lure a victim into a trap which may steal personal and financial information

Beta Testing - Beta testing is a type of user acceptance testing where the product team gives a nearly finished product to a group of target users to evaluate product performance in the real world.

Biometric devices - a device or integration that scans the users biometrics such as finger prints or retina to allow them access to a computer system or device.

BIOS -BIOS (basic input/output system) is the program a computer's microprocessor uses to start the computer system after it is powered on

Black Hat - One of three hacker hats. Black hat hackers gain access to the computer unlawfully with the intent to cause damage or to gain money from the user by holding data at ransom.

Bluetooth - close range wireless frequency used to share files, and connect audio devices for calls and music.

Boolean - data type used where only two options are present to the user. For example; true/false, yes/no or red/black

Botnet - A type of malware that infects the host computer and allows it to be remotely controlled by a botmaster.

C

Cache - Cache memory is a chip-based computer component that makes retrieving data from the computer's memory more efficient. It acts as a temporary storage area that the computer's processor can retrieve data from easily.

Cloud - the umberella term used for describing remote storage of files or access to remote software. Examples include iCloud, Google Cloud or OneDrive

Collaboration tools - Tools within cloud software that allow users in different geographical locations to edit the same document at the same time.

Command Line Interface - known as CLI, this variation of a HCI receive commands from a user in the form of lines of text

CPU - Central Processing Unit, a piece of hardware used to process and execute computer instructions and commands. Often known as the brain of the computer.

D

Data - raw facts and figures with no meaning or context

Database - a database is an organised collection of data stored and accessed electronically.

Decimal - a data type used to represent numbers within code, a spreadsheet or database that have a decimal point.

Diagrammatical representation- The use of computer graphics like graphs and charts to represent data

Dictation - the action of speaking to a device and the device recording it as either sound waves or converting to text. This is known as 'voice to text'.

Digital Communications - the use of technology to communicate information that otherwise would be communicated face to face or via traditional advertisement.

DoS - Denial of Service is a form of malware that is used to shut down a system or website. The attacker floods the device or server with requests which results in it overloading.

E

Email - Electronic mail. Use for communication, allow for attachments as well as advanced controls such as receipts and diary management

Embedded systems - this name is given to computer devices that are a part of a larger system. The embedded device has a primary function and doesn't have any advanced functionalities. Examples include washing machines and cars engine management.

Encryption - Requires a key to unlock the encrypted message. Encryption is a protection method used to keep data secure when shared. Without the key the data remains unreadable.

External Physical Storage - Any storage that is outside/external to the computer/devices core unit.

F

Firewall - A form of defence against malware. Firewalls check incoming traffic from the network and the internet. Anything that cant be verified and may appear dangerous is destroyed on entry. It's like a forcefield!

Flash memory - a form of memory that is faster than magnetic alternatives. Flash memory devices include SSD, Memory Cards and Sticks and RAM

Flow chart - A planning tool used to show any flow/process that will take place. Can be used for code, or user interaciton with a machine.

G

Gesture - In IT this refers to the movement hand or finger to control a device. An example would be swiping your hand across a screen to take a screenshot.

Graphical Tablet - This device has not got a display. It is an input device used for more detailed drawing/sketching/control of a computer. It is an alternative to the mouse

Graphical User Interface - A form of HCI that allows the user to see Windows, Menus, Icons and Pointers, the user uses these features to operate the computer.

H

Hacking - the intention to gain access to a computer system through alternative means, usually without the users/owners knowledge sometimes with the intention to cause damage to the system.

Hard Disk Drive - A form of magnetic storage which has moving platters to store large amounts of data

Hardware - Any aspect of a computer system which is physical and can be 'touched'. Examples include power supply unit, RAM, HDD, SSD, GPU

HCI - Human Computer Interface, the way the user interacts with the copmputer.

I

Icons - A graphical representation, usually a logo or image, which represents something such as a program or file. Used in GUI's.

Identity theft - The stealing of someones identity, often to commit crimes. This could be names and addresses, bank details, or passport information.

Infographics - Visual representation of data that enables the reader/viewer to understand a point of view in more detail. Often used in presentations or posters.

Information - = Data + Meaning + [Context]

Input mask - A way of specifying the format that you want the data entered to appear in when in a database e.g. UK Date Vs. US Date

Integer - A data type used to represent a whole number

Invalid (Erroneous) - A test where you deliberately enter incorrect data to check that the system spots the error

K

Keyboard - an input device to enter data into a system, often text based data
Keypads - Used to enter numerical data for entry into a room, or a ATM/system

L

Legislation - The title given to all of the laws surrounding IT. These laws, when described together, are known as legislation.
Location Based - A location based service only become useable or active when the user is in a specific location. This uses GPS to pinpoint a users device and given them access to location based services.

M

Magnetic Tape - large volume of storage where data is stored linearly. Often used for large data sets that don't need to be used or retrieved often e.g. the census
Magnetic Wipe - the use of an electro-magnet to wipe the data from a magnetic storage device
Malware - malicious software that has the intention to cause damage or harm
Marker Based - a form of AR technology that uses marker points that are prerecorded to display AR visuals to a user when the markers are detected in the camera
Marker less - a form of AR technology that doesn't use marker points. This form of AR randomly places items within the camera window
Menu bar - the name given to the top bar of most software where the user has several drop down menus
Menu Driven Interface - a type of HCI the menu driven interface allows the user to navigate the operating system solely on menus, an example could be an ATM
Microphone - an input device used for sound input
Mind map - planning tool, there are several types of mind maps and different mind maps are appropriate for different scenarios
Mouse - an input device used for inputting data, mice always have a pointer and are used on a GUI

N

Natural Language Interface - the HCI used for voice recognition systems such as Siri, Ask Google and Alexa
Network Attached Storage - centralised storage within a network where one or more device can access the saved material
Non-volatile - The data is not lost when the power source is removed e.g. HDD

O

Object Recognition - using a camera an object is identified when it enters the user viewpoint

Operating system - The software used to navigate the computer system. The OS controls the CPU, memory and the peripherals

P

Peripheral - a name used to describe an item or element outside of the norm. Often used to describe peripheral devices, a peripheral device is a printer or speakers

Phishing - A form of social engineering, phishing intends to 'catch' unsuspecting computer users and get information from them

Physical Destruction - the destroying of data physically such as shredding, or magnetic wipe

Physical prevention methods - ways to protect data and computer systems physically and not logically e.g. a locked door

Pretexting - a social engineering attack where a person pretends to be someone offical when they are not. An example would be a call from Microsoft about your issues, and the person isnt from Microsoft.

Q

Quid pro quo - Quid pro quo is a kind of social engineering attack where a hacker promises a profit in exchange for information that can later be used to steal money, data, or take control of a user account on a website.

R

Radio-frequency identification (RFID) - Radio-frequency identification uses electromagnetic fields to automatically identify and track tags attached to objects.

RAM - Random-access memory is a form of computer memory that can be read and changed in any order, typically used to store working data and machine code.

Ransomware - Ransomware is a type of malware that threatens to publish the victim's personal data or perpetually block access to it unless a ransom is paid.

Real-Time Collaboration - A collaborative real-time editor is a type of collaboration software or web application which enables real-time collaborative editing

Regression Testing - Regression testing is a software testing practice that ensures an application still functions as expected after any code changes, updates, or improvements

ROM - Read-only memory is a type of non-volatile memory used in computers and other electronic devices

S

Scareware - Scareware is a form of malware which uses social engineering to cause shock, anxiety, or the perception of a threat in order to manipulate users into buying unwanted software.

Shoulder Surfing - shoulder surfing is a type of social engineering technique used to obtain information such as personal identification numbers, passwords and other confidential data by looking over the victim's shoulder

Solid State Drive - A solid-state drive (SSD) is a solid-state storage device that uses integrated circuit assemblies to store data persistently, typically using flash memory

Spyware - Spyware is a type of malicious software or malware that is installed on a computing device without the end user's knowledge.

Storage - Software is a set of instructions, data or programs used to operate computers and execute specific tasks.

Stress Testing - Stress testing is a software testing activity that determines the robustness of software by testing beyond the limits of normal operation

T

Telephony - Telephony is the field of technology involving the development, application, and deployment of telecommunication/phones.

Touch screen - an input device that allows the user to interact with a GUI using their finger as an input

Trojan horse - a form of malware a Trojan horse is any malware that misleads users of its true intent.

Two Factor Authentication (2FA) - 2FA authentication is an electronic authentication method in which a user is granted access to a website or application only after successfully presenting two or more pieces of evidence to an authentication mechanism

U

UI - User Interface means the way in which the user uses the device

V

Validation - Validation is the name given to the process whereby the information entered into a database is checked to ensure that it makes sense.

Visualisation diagrams - used to plan out how digital artefacts will looks such as presentations, leaflets and flyers

VoIP - Voice over internet protocol is used for internet calls and video calls such as Facetime, Skype, WhatsApp

Volatile - when the power is removed all data will be lost. 'RAM is volatile'

W

Wearables - *Any form of technology that can be worn by a person. Examples include, Smart Watches, Smart Rings, GPRS Tracking devices, Headphones etc.*

White Hat - *One of the three hacking hats, white hat hackers have permission to hack the system and are doing it to find 'holes' that could be exploited maliciously. Sometimes known as ethical hackers or cyber security engineers*

WiFi *-A form of wireless connectivity that can be used within short ranges to connect devices to the internet.*

WIMP- *Windows Icons Menus Pointers - the way we interact with a HCI*

Wireframe diagram - *A graphic representation of a website or application*

Wireless Network Drive - *A form of storage which can be wirelessly accessed from within a single local area network.*

Worm - *A piece of malware a computer worm is a standalone malware computer program that replicates itself in order to spread to other computers.*

Index

3

3D · 74, 75, 79, 80, 81, 84

4

4G · 63, 65, 66

5

5G · 63, 65, 66

A

Access rights · 51
Action Flow · 86
Adware · 48
Alpha Testing · 43
Alphanumeric · 37
Anti-virus · 51
App · 14, 22, 31, 32, 33, 64, 71, 72
Applications · 12, 21, 73
AR in applications · 5, 82
AR in Education · 4, 76
AR in lifestyle · 5, 80
AR in Movies/TV and Film · 78
AR in Retail · 5, 79
Architects · 12
Assistive technology · 21
Assistive Technology · 24
Audio · 59
Augmented Reality · 4, 5, 74, 76, 77, 78, 79, 80, 83, 84
Augmented Reality in the Entertainment Industry · 4, 77

B

Baiting · 47
Beta Testing · 43
Biometric devices · 50
BIOS · 26
Black Hat · 45
Bluetooth · 65
Boolean · 37
botnet · 48

C

Cache · 27
Cache memory · 25, 27
Cloud · 40, 64
Coaxial cables · 67
Collaboration tools · 60
Command Line Interface · 16
Computer Misuse Act 1990 · 53
Copyright Designs and Patents Act · 55
CPU · 20, 25, 27, 29, 30
Currency · 37

D

Data · 27, 28, 29, 36, 37, 38, 39, 42, 49, 52, 53, 54, 58, 67, 71
Data collection methods · 39
Database · 31, 33
Date · 37
Decimal · 37
Diagrammatical representation · 6, 7, 60
Dictation · 21
Digital Communications · 59
DoS · 49
Drop down list · 38

E

Email · 39, 64
Embedded Applications · 21
Embedded systems · 14
Encryption · 52
External Physical Storage · 41
Extreme · 42

F

Facility Operations and Maintenance · 75
Fibre cabling · 69
Firewalls · 51
Flash memory · 25, 27, 28
Flow chart · 6, 7
Format check · 38
Freedom of Information Act 2000 · 56

G

GDPR · 49, 53, 54
Gesture · 35
Government Statistics · 39
Graphical Tablet · 23
Graphical User Interface · 16, 20, 23
Grey Hat · 45

H

Hacking · 45, 46
Hard Disk Drive · 28, 41
Hardware · 16
HCI · 13, 14, 15, 16, 21, 22, 23, 24, 29, 30, 31, 32, 33, 34, 35, 43, 72
HDD · 20, 28, 41
Health and Safety at Work Act 2000 · 57
High definition · 29
Hotspot · 66
Human interaction · 13, 14, 72
Hyperlinks · 34

I

Icons · 14, 35
Identity theft · 49
Infographics · 60
Information · 7, 8, 9, 10, 11, 12, 21, 23, 25, 30, 32, 34, 35, 36, 40, 44, 47, 48, 49, 51, 54, 56, 58, 60, 61, 62, 64, 66, 70, 71, 73
Input mask · 38
Integer · 37
Integration Testing · 43
Interaction · 13, 15, 16, 20, 23, 24, 32, 35, 72
Internet of Everything · 70, 71
Invalid (Erroneous) · 42
IoE · 70, 71, 72, 73

K

Keyboard · 23, 35
Keypads · 50

L

Legislation · 53, 58
Length check · 38
Library · 7, 8, 9

Library mind maps · 8
Limited choice · 38
Location Based · 84
Lookup · 38

M

Magnetic Tape · 28
Magnetic Wipe · 52
Malware · 48, 51
Marker Based · 83
Marker less · 83, 84
Memory · 25, 27, 28, 30, 41
Menu bar · 19, 34
Menu Driven interface · 16, 23, 35
Menu Driven Interface · 18, 33, 35
Menus · 14, 35
Microphone · 23, 35
Mind map · 7, 8, 9
Mobile App · 32
Monitor · 22
Mouse · 23, 35
MS-DOS · 16

N

Natural Language Interface · 16, 21, 23, 35
Network Attached Storage · 41
Non-volatile · 25, 27
Numeric · 37

O

Object Recognition · 83
Office of National Statistics · 39
Operating system · 20, 22, 26, 30, 31, 41
Operating Systems · 12, 30
OS · 30

P

Percentage · 37
Peripheral · 22, 23, 30
Permissions · 51
Phishing · 47
Physical Destruction · 52
Physical prevention methods · 50

Physical storage · 41
Pointers · 14
Presence check · 38
Presentation · 7, 9
Presentation mind map · 9
Pretexting · 47
Preventing Threats · 50
Primary Hard Drive · 41
primary storage · 25, 26
Project Planning · 75

Q

Quid pro quo · 47

R

Radio buttons · 38
Radio-frequency identification (RFID) · 50
RAM · 25, 26, 27, 29
Range check · 38
Ransomware · 48
Real-Time Collaboration · 75
Regression Testing · 43
ROM · 25, 26

S

Sat Nav · 14
Scareware · 47
Secure backups · 51
Security · 30, 49, 73
Shoulder Surfing · 48
Smart watch · 14, 73
Social engineering · 47, 51
Social media · 61
Social Media · 39, 61
Solid State Drive · 28
Spreadsheet · 33
Spyware · 48
SSD · 27, 28, 41
Static · 34, 86
Static designs · 10
Storage · 25, 26, 27, 28, 29, 30, 33, 40, 41, 51, 64
Stress Testing · 43
Superimposed · 83, 85
system requirements · 29

T

Telephony · 21, 69
Test data · 42
testing · 36, 42, 43
Text · 37
Tick list · 38
Touch · 22, 35
Touch screen · 22
trojan horse · 48
tunnel timeline · 8
Tunnel timeline · 7
Two Factor Authentication (2FA) · 51

U

UI · 12
Underground Construction · 75
Unit Testing · 43
Usernames and Passwords · 52
Uses of AR in Architecture · 75
Utilities · 30

V

Valid · 42
Validation · 38, 42
Video · 39, 62
Virus · 45, 47, 48, 51
Visualisation diagrams · 10
Voice · 35, 63
VoIP · 63, 64, 65
Volatile · 25, 26, 27, 28

W

Wearables · 21, 73
Websites · 12, 33, 39, 64, 73
White Hat · 45, 46
WiFi · 66, 73
WIMP · 14
Windows · 14, 20, 29, 30, 35
Wireframe diagram · 12
Wireframes · 12
Wireless Network Drives · 41
Workflow · 6
Worm · 48, 51

Printed in Great Britain
by Amazon